# SURGE

**Amith Prabhu** is a pioneering Public Relations and reputation management professional with over twenty years of experience. He has worked in India and in the USA at leading marketing communication companies. He is the co-founder of India's only weekend offsite summit for the profession, PRAXIS. He serves on the international board of the Global Alliance (GA). He is the founding dean at the School of Communications & Reputation (SCoRe) in Mumbai. He has a postgraduate degree in Public Relations and communication management from Symbiosis Institute of Media and Communication. He lives in Gurgaon. He can be found on Twitter @amithpr.

**Sarika Chavan** is the founder of Sparkle Gift Cards and the director of social impact at The PRomise Foundation. She is a Public Relations professional with over nineteen years of work experience. Her last stint was at Weber Shandwick Mumbai, where she was vice president—client experience. Previously she was employed at Adfactors PR, Text100 (now known as Archetype) and Perfect Relations. She writes the longest-running monthly book review column. She has a postgraduate diploma in PR from the Xavier Institute of Communications and a postgraduate diploma in marketing from the Welingkar Institute of Management. She lives in Mumbai. She can be found on Twitter @sourikka.

EDITED BY
**AMITH PRABHU**
AND
**SARIKA CHAVAN**

# SURGE

STORIES AND INSIGHTS FROM INDIA'S LEADING CHIEF COMMUNICATIONS OFFICERS

WESTLAND
**BUSINESS**

**WESTLAND**
**BUSINESS**

Published by Westland Business, an imprint of Westland Books, a division of Nasadiya Technologies Private Limited, in 2025

No. 269/2B, First Floor, 'Irai Arul', Vimalraj Street, Nethaji Nagar, Alapakkam Main Road, Maduravoyal, Chennai 600095

Westland, the Westland logo, Westland Business and the Westland Business logo are the trademarks of Nasadiya Technologies Private Limited, or its affiliates.

Copyright © Amith Prabhu and Sarika Chavan, 2025

ISBN: 9789371974493

10 9 8 7 6 5 4 3 2 1

The views and opinions expressed in this work are the authors' own and the facts are as reported by them, and the publisher is in no way liable for the same.

All rights reserved

Typeset by Mukul

Printed at Manipal Technologies Limited, Manipal

No part of this book may be reproduced, or stored in a retrieval system, or transmitted in any form or by any means, electronic, mechanical, photocopying, recording, or otherwise, without express written permission of the publisher.

*We dedicate this book to every fellow professional in Indian Public Relations, whether in corporate communications or in consultancy, the profession surges ahead because of their contribution to it.*

# Contents

*Introduction* ix

1. Amrit Ahuja 1
2. Arpana Ahuja 5
3. Seema Ahuja 11
4. Nazeeb Arif 17
5. Sanjay Arora 23
6. Melissa Arulappan 27
7. Roma Balwani 31
8. Rohit Bansal 35
9. Sudeep Bhalla 42
10. Ophira Bhatia 46
11. Nandini Chatterjee 51
12. Paresh Chaudhry 55
13. Paroma Roy Chowdhury 61
14. Madhu Chhibber 66
15. Shravani Dang 70
16. Anuj Dayal 75
17. Deepa Dey 80
18. Meenu Handa 85
19. Mahesh Jayaram 91

| | | |
|---|---|---|
| 20. | Ritu Jhingon | 97 |
| 21. | Narahari K.S. | 101 |
| 22. | Bharatendu Kabi | 107 |
| 23. | Manish Kalghatgi | 114 |
| 24. | Himanshu Kapadia | 117 |
| 25. | Sanjiv Kataria | 121 |
| 26. | Raza Khan | 127 |
| 27. | Alpana Killawala | 132 |
| 28. | Rakhee Lalvani | 138 |
| 29. | Nivedeeta Moirangthem | 143 |
| 30. | Subhayu Mishra | 146 |
| 31. | Rachana Panda | 151 |
| 32. | Sujit Patil | 156 |
| 33. | Ramya Rajagopalan | 160 |
| 34. | Mukund Rajan | 166 |
| 35. | Senjam Raj Sekhar | 175 |
| 36. | Pragnya Ram | 180 |
| 37. | Debasis Ray | 183 |
| 38. | Minari Shah | 187 |
| 39. | Amandeep Singh | 193 |
| 40. | Atul Takle | 199 |
| 41. | Nitin Thakur | 205 |
| 42. | Aparna Thomas | 211 |
| 43. | Varghese Thomas | 217 |
| 44. | Aman Ullah | 222 |
| 45. | Shaily Vaswani | 228 |
| 46. | Pradeep Wadhwa | 233 |

*Afterword*     237

# Introduction

The trilogy is now complete with *Surge* in your hands. This book is a collection of stories from forty-six professionals. Make sure to get a copy of the first two books, *Spark* and *Shine*, if you haven't already.

With this magnum opus we have stories of a few handpicked fellow professionals. There will always be debates and discussions as to why some names did not feature or why some names featured. We researched over a hundred names and arrived at over fifty-five current and former chief communications officers (CCOs). We felt they all had a story to tell that would inspire present and future practitioners. A few declined to be part of the project and a few others did not respond. And that is how we have this collection of first-person accounts.

A note by these luminaries will also feature on lightaspark. online where one may read their perspectives. We hope this repository of knowledge works for different people in different ways. To start with, these are the stories of storytellers. Most of these current and former CCOs have spent a lifetime helping companies, brands and business leaders surge ahead with their strategies. They may have never come forward with their story because they have oriented themselves towards being backroom players. But their life sketches need to be recorded as there is much to learn from them.

The book is a collection of campaigns, anecdotes and tales from corporate India that will be an interesting read whether you are student, a working professional or a homemaker. There is a treasure trove of trivia that can help produce a series of quizzes. And there is scope to convert some of these stories into documentaries.

We hope you enjoy reading the book and share your feedback with the authors or reach out to the individuals to tell them directly on social media what struck a chord.

# 1

# Amrit Ahuja

FORMER DIRECTOR - COMMUNICATIONS,
FACEBOOK INDIA

---

*'My journey from a young girl dreaming of riding a shikara to a professional navigating the intersections of communication, social impact and personal transformation has been very exciting and fulfilling.'*

GROWING UP AS AN ARMY KID MEANT THAT MY CHILDHOOD was filled with frequent travel, adapting to new cities and new schools. I was four years old when I started school after a brief stint in playschool in Delhi. My father was posted in Srinagar at the time, and I attended Presentation Convent School there. I remember envying my classmates who arrived in elegant shikaras as their homes were situated along the Dal Lake.

Srinagar's political climate made everyday life unpredictable. Curfews and sudden school closures were common. I vividly recall one such day when school was abruptly closed and the phone lines were jammed. Unable to contact my parents, my teacher invited me to her home and offered to take me there by shikara. I leapt at the opportunity, thrilled to finally experience the shikara ride that had always fascinated me. Meanwhile, my parents were frantic. Oblivious to the panic back home, I simply enjoyed the journey. My father mobilised an army patrol to search for me, complete with loudspeakers announcing my description. Eventually, my teacher heard the commotion and flagged them down. Though I was safely returned home, my mother was inconsolable. That incident compelled my parents to move into a rented house in the city to ease the commute and ensure my safety.

The new home was idyllic—a charming house nestled in an orchard surrounded by apple trees. Those early years in Srinagar left a lasting impression on me. I grew deeply attached to its scenic beauty, rich handicrafts and cuisine, a connection that endures to this day.

Initially, I aspired to become a doctor, but life had other plans. A chance meeting with a PR professional from ONGC introduced me to the field. Her encouragement led me to pursue a degree in English from Hansraj College, followed by a diploma in advertising and PR. My career began with ITDC, where I organised glamorous events and hosted journalists, an exciting start for a twenty-one-year-old.

Marriage brought me to Bombay, and motherhood soon followed. I chose to dedicate a decade to raising my children, though I stayed connected to the profession, occasionally interviewing for roles but prioritising my family. Eventually, when my younger child began playschool, I felt ready to re-enter the workforce. My first step back was unconventional—I walked into a nearby hotel and offered to help. This experience gave me the confidence to balance work and home life.

A chance connection through a colleague at the hotel led me to Zee Network in 1994, the year Zee entered the Indian market. Joining their PR team marked the true restart of my career in communications, setting the stage for everything that followed. Satellite television was a novel concept at the time, marking a significant departure from the dominance of Doordarshan.

It was an exhilarating time for me, as I was deeply involved in launching new channels almost daily. My work put me at the centre of vibrant content creation. The office was abuzz with excitement, frequented by television stars, teeming with creative proposals and offering a front-row seat to evaluating what content worked for TV. That was when Zee partnered with Star TV, adhering to strict content guidelines. This collaborative environment was a fertile ground for learning and innovation.

After two thrilling years at Zee, my husband, an oil engineer, was transferred to Delhi, where I joined Zee's news division. The slower pace and newsroom hierarchy, dominated by Rajat Sharma, felt worlds apart from the dynamic and creative environment I had left behind. Realising I needed to pursue something more aligned with my aspirations, I decided to explore PR firms.

Rejecting offers from reputed firms like Mudra and Genesis, I joined a relatively unknown technology PR firm, 2020 Media, as its fourth employee. The decision was unconventional, and my family, especially my in-laws, were sceptical. They had enjoyed introducing me as the glamorous 'daughter-in-law who works at Zee', and my switch to a small firm puzzled them. However, I trusted my instincts and the vision of the founder, Sunil Agarwal, who offered me the flexibility I needed as a mother of two.

This decision turned out to be a game changer. At 2020 Media, I witnessed the transformative power of technology PR. From working with industry giants like Intel, HP and Google to navigating the digital revolution, my career flourished. Over twenty-three years, I contributed to the firm's growth from a start-up to a mid-sized company and later through its acquisition by Publicis Groupe.

Eventually, I transitioned to Meta, where I served as the communications director for Instagram, WhatsApp and Facebook during India's first digital elections. This phase offered rich experiences but also exposed me to the darker sides of the internet, prompting a re-evaluation of my career path.

In 2019, I shifted focus to the social sector, joining the Michael & Susan Dell Foundation. The onset of COVID-19 redirected my role towards enhancing digital communication for non-profits. Since then, I have worked with UNICEF, Central Square Foundation and other organisations, leveraging my expertise to amplify their impact through compelling storytelling.

My journey from a young girl dreaming of riding a shikara to a professional navigating the intersections of communication, social impact and personal transformation has been very exciting and fulfilling.

# 2

# Arpana Ahuja

## EVP & Head - Corporate Brand & Communications, Jindal Steel & Power Ltd

*'Early on, some experiences taught me one of my biggest life lessons—always have a Plan B.'*

I WAS BORN IN CHENNAI, THE YOUNGEST OF THREE CHILDREN, to parents who deeply valued education and adaptability. My father served in the Indian Air Force. I credit my mother for instilling in me the importance of learning.

Being the youngest, I looked up to my two older sisters too, who were strong role models in their own right. Fortunately, my parents never imposed career choices on us—they encouraged independence and exploration. My goal was clear: complete my English Honours degree and secure admission to the Indian Institute of Mass Communication (IIMC). At that time, IIMC was the gold standard, and I never considered a backup plan. However, fate had other plans. The day before my IIMC entrance exam, I fell severely ill with food poisoning and had to be hospitalised. Unable to take the exam, I was devastated. Back then, taking a gap year was unheard of, and I had no contingency plan. That experience taught me one of my biggest life lessons—always have a Plan B.

I then applied to Xavier's Institute of Communications (XIC) and made it. Jane Swamy, who ran the programme, explained to me that for an advanced course, work experience was a pre-requisite. I found a role at Exponential Consultants, a small but dynamic consultancy run by two enterprising women, Meraj Naqvi and Satnam Sachdeva. They became my first mentors—strong, enabling women who shaped my career.

Exponential Consultants handled direct marketing and PR with clients like Indage India, which was launching the Marquise De Pompadour champagne in India, and the Fariyas Hotels group. I was brought on primarily for Fariyas, which was undergoing a relaunch after a change in ownership.

Looking back, my work at Fariyas was my first exposure to what we now call influencer management. Back then, Magna Publishing was the go-to for luxury, lifestyle and travel coverage, and my job involved organising familiarisation trips, experiential campaigns and media outreach—skills that would prove invaluable throughout my career.

That was 1993 and the year changed me profoundly. I had the opportunity to continue working in Mumbai but my parents were concerned about unrest in the city and urged me to return to Delhi. At the same time, maintaining a long-distance relationship with my now-husband, who was in Delhi, was not easy. So, I decided to move back.

Back in Delhi, I joined Prema Sagar. While I was keen on PR, she convinced me to take on a project close to her heart—*Genesis, the City Guide*. Long before Genesis PR, she had launched this magazine, a precursor to *Time Out*, which was distributed in hotels and major travel agencies, including

ITDC properties. She hired me as the marketing and PR manager, effectively making me one of two key people running it alongside the editor. After a year, though, I was eager to shift fully into PR.

That's when Good Relations offered me a compelling opportunity, which I accepted. Good Relations was one of the most well-connected and well-funded consultancies of its time—the precursor to today's global network consultancies. With Anthony B. Good overseeing operations from London, we handled many international clients, particularly those entering India during the liberalisation era. Our work spanned telecom, insurance (Sun Life, later acquired by Apollo Munich) and several other sectors.

From Good Relations, I was headhunted by Clea PR, which was at its peak at the time. It was a bold, maverick consultancy. At Clea PR, I eventually became the branch head. Those were exhilarating days. I was handling accounts such as Channel [V] Music Awards and international superstars like Madonna, Bryan Adams and the Spice Girls when they performed in India. It was a thrilling ride. Then, in 2000, everything came to a sudden halt. I had a serious accident that left me with a back broken in three places. I was bedridden, facing a long recovery. So, I took a break.

*Encyclopaedia Britannica* had been one of my clients at Clea PR. When they heard I was leaving, they offered me a position. I explained my health situation, and to my surprise, they were incredibly accommodating. They assured me they would make adjustments and give me the flexibility I needed. True to their word, they set up my workspace to ensure my comfort—long before workplace accommodations became a topic of discussion.

I joined Britannica at an exciting time. We were a small team of about ten, and there was a new, ambitious owner who was focused on the digital revolution. It was the first dot-com wave, and the entire Britannica archive was being digitised in India. The transition was massive, and I found myself right at the centre of it.

One of the landmark achievements during this time was the launch of *Students' Britannica*, the first-ever country-specific product in *Encyclopaedia Britannica*'s history. Until then, Britannica had been a globally uniform product, but this edition was tailored specifically for India. It was a moment of immense pride when it was launched by the president of India. Being involved in product development, collaborating with the editorial team and contributing to Britannica.com and Britannica.co.in—all centred around the Indian context—was a career high.

When my daughter was born, I faced the dilemma many women experience—balancing motherhood and a career. I had seen my sisters navigate this challenge, but I knew I did not want a routine where I barely got to see my child, dropping her off at my parents' house in the morning and picking her up late at night. That did not sit well with me. So, my husband and I decided that I would take a break and focus on being a hands-on mother.

However, within a month, I realised something—I deeply loved my daughter but I also needed something more. That's when another pivotal woman entered my life, Archana Jain. I had known her since my days at Genesis, and she had always been a mentor and a friend. When she visited to bless my child, we started talking about my restlessness. She suggested various ideas, and a week later, she called me with an offer: 'Why don't you work for me?'

I hesitated, explaining my challenges—being a new mother, the logistics and the commitments. She suggested we try a flexible arrangement—come in for a few hours, work remotely and see if it worked for both of us. We agreed to a three-month trial. That trial turned into fifteen years.

PR Pundit became my creative playground. While I had already gained experience in growing businesses—first as a branch head in Clea PR, then in Britannica's management—at PR Pundit, I was building something alongside Archana. I played a key role in the consultancy's brand identity, strategic expansion and the creation of bespoke training models. One of my proudest contributions was launching and developing PR Pundit's social and digital suite, which has since become one of its strongest assets.

At PR Pundit, I eventually reached a point where I asked myself, 'What next?' The firm had grown into a leading player in the luxury and consumer lifestyle space but I felt my personal growth was beginning to plateau. That's when Weber Shandwick happened. I was curious to see what an international network consultancy looked like. It was not an easy decision—leaving a place I had invested fifteen years in. But I knew I needed a new challenge.

Weber Shandwick gave me a broader perspective into handling global mandates, understanding regional and global priorities and navigating the dynamics of a network consultancy. I also gained a deeper appreciation for the business side of communications: profitability, cross-cultural collaboration and working across geographies.

But just as I was settling in, Shell came knocking. Curiosity led me to explore the opportunity. Unlike my previous jobs, which had precipitated through referrals, this was a structured hiring process—with case studies, group discussions and multiple rounds of evaluations. It was a new experience, and honestly, a bit thrilling to clear each stage.

It was also a period of massive transformation. It was the time of the pandemic, Ukraine war, global energy transition. India, with the largest Shell employee base, played a crucial role in shaping the company's narrative.

Beyond communications, Shell deepened my commitment to mentoring, diversity and inclusion. I was able to drive these agendas with passion, particularly through employee resource groups, which was immensely satisfying.

Now, at Jindal Steel, I find myself in yet another new industry—steel, the backbone of infrastructure.

Joining Jindal at a pivotal time, I was tasked with sustaining the momentum of their first-ever corporate brand campaign, 'Steel of India'. A key challenge was strengthening the employer brand, leading to the creation of 'Mettle of India' as an extension of that narrative.

Across decades and industries, I have realised one truth: communication is about connection. My leadership style is rooted in empathy, clarity and action. I believe in building cultures where people can thrive and where purpose fuels performance.

At every turn, I have chosen curiosity over comfort, values over velocity. That, I believe, is the real story.

# 3

# Seema Ahuja

### SVP & Global Head - Communications & Corporate Brand, Biocon Group & Biocon Biologics

*'I learnt early on how to balance my personal and professional life without sacrificing one for the other.'*

I WAS BORN IN DELHI IN A DEVOUT SIKH PUNJABI FAMILY with a deep spiritual grounding. My father migrated from present-day Pakistan when he was just about thirteen years old. My mother was born in Punjab. Sadly, I did not get much time to live with my parents and was raised by my grandparents.

I'm proud to be the first woman in my family to work, as previous generations of women in our family were more devoted to religious pursuits.

I sat for the highly competitive national entrance exams for the Institute of Hotel Management (IHM), which I cleared and joined IHM Pusa, New Delhi, where I completed a three-year programme in Hotel Management, Catering and

Nutrition. It was an exhaustive programme that not only taught the topics related to the hotel industry but also general management, marketing, advertising, law and communications besides English and French as languages. While studying, we also worked with various five-star hotels, providing banquet services and other guest services.

In 1989, I was in my final year of hotel management. During campus interviews, I was selected by the first hotel that interviewed me—Sofitel Surya, a French hotel chain that had just opened in South Delhi. While most of my friends were pursuing roles in housekeeping, I was very clear that I wanted to be in the front office, interacting with guests. During my interview, however, the managing director of the hotel told me that I should not limit myself to front office or guest relations but rather focus on hotel sales and marketing, where I could do very well.

Taking his advice, I joined Sofitel Surya as a management trainee in the sales department along with a small group of college mates who joined different departments. That was the beginning of my journey in hospitality, where I learnt about customer service, guest relations and the importance of creating a positive experience for anyone who walked through our doors. There was a certain power and influence that came with that role.

During that time, I worked with several big clients, including what is now Airtel, Ranbaxy, Max Group, Apollo Tyres, Modi Xerox. Eventually, I moved on to Hotel Imperial for a sales and marketing manager's role, heading the department. Besides direct corporate sales, I was also responsible for marketing the hotel, which meant working out special promotional packages, working with travel agencies, conceptualising events. This role allowed me to step into a leadership position, and it was then that I realised that sales and marketing were truly my calling.

Around this time, I got married and moved from South Delhi to North Delhi, which needed a big adjustment, but I embraced it. Working in the hotel industry meant long hours—since during the day, I'd meet with clients, handling sales calls, and in the evening, there were always events to oversee. This twelve-hour workday routine began with my first job and continued throughout my career.

Later, I joined Oberoi Hotels. Initially, I was interviewed for the hotel sales and marketing function, but the head of HR liked my profile so much that they offered me a role with the legendary P.R.S. Oberoi, in the chairman's office.

After my son was born, I took a sabbatical from the Oberoi Group but did not stop working. During that time, I worked as a consultant on various projects. One of the major projects was for Lintas, where I did market research for a leading brand. I also helped launch Village Bistro, a unique restaurant complex in Hauz Khas Village, New Delhi, which had live Rajasthani musicians and dancers and offered multiple speciality dining experiences in a Rajasthani setting across their different outlets.

When I decided to return to the Oberoi Group, I was offered a sales job at the Oberoi in Bangalore but due to family priorities at that time, I could not take up the job since it was outside Delhi and had to resign. I started exploring opportunities to get back into a hardcore corporate job and that was when I was introduced to the world of PR and corporate communications.

Through a friend in a leading publishing house, who was also an ex-client, I was introduced to Ranjana Smetacek, who had just joined Ranbaxy as the head of corporate communications, and she was looking to build her team.

During my tenure at Ranbaxy from 1996 to 2007, I learnt a great deal about crisis communication, brand management, digital communication, information technology, finance, internal audit and employee communication. Overall, my experience at Ranbaxy was incredibly enriching, allowing me to grow in the field of corporate communications while making meaningful contributions to the organisation.

In 1999, Ranjana decided to move on. This left me in charge of managing the department for about a year until they found a replacement. I continued with the company till 2007 as general manager, but I wanted to become the head of the department. I did not see that opportunity coming my way at Ranbaxy, so I decided to explore opportunities outside the company.

Lupin Pharma based in Mumbai reached out to me and I saw it as a good opportunity. Though it meant leaving my city and a company where I had built a strong reputation and personal connections, I knew it was time to take the next step and finally made the tough decision of leaving Ranbaxy.

When I met Chairman D.B. Gupta (DBG), who was also the MD and CEO, it became clear that Lupin had all the potential to be seen as a global pharmaceutical giant, at par with companies like Dr Reddy's or Ranbaxy at that time. The company had all the fundamentals of a leading pharma company but lacked any PR or reputation building strategy. Their story had not been effectively communicated, and they needed someone to help build that reputation. This challenge of repositioning Lupin was what drew me to the role.

After completing my commitments at Lupin, I eventually moved back to Delhi and began the next chapter of life with Jubilant Organosys as vice president, corporate marketing and communications.

In my more than three years at Jubilant, one of the best compliments I received was when many people in the organisation told me that what I had achieved in three years was more than what had been done in the company in the past thirty years. It was a validation of the impact I had made with the quality of work I had put in to build a reputation for Jubilant Life Sciences and the Jubilant Bhartia group.

Subsequently, I was approached by an ex-colleague from Jubilant who had moved to Biocon. He was greatly impressed with the work I had done at Jubilant Group and believed Biocon could immensely benefit from a professional like me. He encouraged me to meet the leadership team.

During my time in the pharma industry, I knew Biocon as one of the API suppliers of Ranbaxy. So, when I was first approached for Biocon, I was hesitant to consider it, but the head of talent acquisition at Biocon pursued me for a long time, asking me to visit Bangalore once and meet Kiran Mazumdar-Shaw.

At our first meeting, Kiran did not ask me a single question about my past work. When her secretary informed her about the next meeting, I pointed out that we hadn't discussed my professional experience. She simply replied, 'If you've worked with Ranbaxy and with Mr Brar and Dr Singh for over a decade, I don't need to question your competency.' She expressed that she saw a lot of potential for us to work together to elevate brand Biocon's reputation, which resonated well with me.

In December 2011, I joined Biocon. What attracted me to Biocon was the opportunity to work in biotech, having worked in pharma and the life sciences industry for nearly two decades. It seemed like a great progression from a sector perspective, moving up the value chain from small molecules to large molecules. It offered avenues for new learning.

In many ways, my years with Biocon echo my experience at Ranbaxy—crafting a brand's voice on the global stage. Whether as a pioneering global pharma brand for Ranbaxy or a pioneering global biotech brand for Biocon, my career has been driven by a desire to elevate the company and industry's profile, empower people and inspire new standards of excellence. Through our strategic work across Biocon's business verticals—Generics, Biosimilars, Research Services (Syngene) and Novels—we have built a narrative based on pioneering research and a vision that reflects the unique strengths of each brand.

This journey has been a fulfilling one, and I look forward to all the ways I can continue to make a larger impact.

# 4

# Nazeeb Arif

EVP & Chief - Corporate Communications, ITC Limited

---

*'The perfect childhood in Assam and the pragmatic fast-moving world of Delhi shaped my perspective and laid the foundation of my career.'*

I GREW UP IN ASSAM AND SHILLONG, WHICH IS NOW PART OF Meghalaya. The life we led is something people would pay a fortune for today. I grew up surrounded by pristine nature, rooted in deep relationships, a close-knit extended family, travelling across terrains unimagined and experiencing a rich cultural environment. The most invaluable part of growing up was experiencing the world in its purest form. Life was simple, certainly not extravagant, but incredibly rich in experiences and values.

My parents played a huge role in shaping my worldview. My father, Arif Ali, was in the IAS. As he grew from roles in sub-divisions and districts of Assam to New Delhi as commissioner and secretary in many departments and as the chairperson of innumerable state corporations, eventually retiring as the chairman of the Assam Public Service Commission, our life too got enriched with a tremendous variety of experiences and connections with people from a diverse world. He was a man of high integrity and, even decades after his passing, people still remember him as an extremely upright, honest and capable administrator. That sense of integrity was ingrained in us from a young age.

My mother was a homemaker, the life and soul of our family. You could call her an epitome of PR. She could relate to anyone irrespective of age, culture or background, was a go-to person for everyone and very lively and cheerful, always bursting with energy. She was extremely creative as a writer and penned many stories in Assamese, though she could also write in Bengali.

Given that my parents were both public figures in one way or the other, it certainly influenced my growing years, and the career I stepped into first was in economic policy advocacy. My father's role meant that we grew up amidst government dignitaries giving us the privilege of meeting the then presidents, prime ministers, chief ministers, ministers and senior bureaucrats. In fact, when we were in school in the state capital, Dispur, my room used to open up to the road outside and it was then common for even the chief minister and other dignitaries to walk to their offices, which was near my campus. They would see us studying and talk to us about what we were doing, what we found interesting and what we wanted to do in life. As a result, meeting and conversing with such high-level public figures was something that came very naturally to me. There was no sense of awe or intimidation around authoritative figures—we saw them as people, not just their titles. That exposure was immensely helpful when I pursued a career first in the Chamber of Commerce, which required a lot of understanding of public policy and significant interactions with the government on policy matters. It also came in handy while interacting with leaders, government officials and global figures later in my professional life.

My schooling began at St Edmund's and continued in Shillong until Class 6. With my father's transfers, I moved through several schools, including Carmel in Jorhat, before finally completing my Class 10 at Don Bosco in Guwahati. From there, I attended the prestigious Cotton College, Guwahati—now Cotton University—for my pre-university education. My academic journey then took me to Delhi University, where I pursued BA (Hons) in Economics followed by a Masters in Business Economics.

After graduating, I worked on a World Bank project and was later selected to join FICCI, the apex industry association, followed by the Indian Chamber of Commerce and eventually ITC. When serving in FICCI, I had a variety of experiences and had mentors who gave me phenomenal insight into the working of the chambers. The work and exposure was not only interesting but completely aligned to what I wanted to do. Therefore, it was not very surprising that in my fifth year at FICCI, I was given the challenge to modernise a regional chamber, the Indian Chamber of Commerce (ICC), which was one of the founders of FICCI during India's freedom movement. That was how I reached Kolkata, now my home for thirty-three years, perhaps one of the best phases of my life. The task to transform ICC was immensely motivating, and I was passionate about what I was doing. In 1994, the organisation announced my elevation to the position of secretary-general and CEO. I was thirty-two, I believe the youngest to hold this position in the organisation's history, and took on a responsibility that became my life 24x7. I found myself working closely with leaders, multilateral institutions and policymakers. It was a dynamic environment that required agility, adaptability and a deep understanding of economic and business policies.

This exposure to economic policy, business advocacy and stakeholder engagement provided a unique perspective and an ability to communicate effectively and build relationships—both essential skills in the world of corporate communications.

During my time in the chambers, I learnt five key things:

1. *The influence of an honest message*: The importance of clarity and integrity in communication
2. *The strength of conviction*: Passion drives credibility, making messages more impactful
3. *The ability to navigate change*: The 1991 economic reforms and subsequent shifts in India's business landscape provided a first-hand view of transformation
4. *The power of people*: At the heart of achieving anything is a great team, a knowledgeable and influential ecosystem and superior relationships with all stakeholders
5. *The differentiator in innovation*: The winning edge lies in innovation and is the only way to be ahead of the curve.

And then one day, at a dinner, Y.C. Deveshwar, the then chairman of ITC, asked if I would like to join ITC and help contribute to this exemplary enterprise's journey to build an institution of national pride. At that point, I had already been a CEO for several years, was completely invested in building ICC's future and was not keen on anything else.

However, this opportunity offered something different—the chance to translate broad macro insights into real-world corporate action, work with a corporate legend and learn a completely new world of strategy, brands and business excellence. ITC's vision of sustainability and nation-building resonated deeply with me. I eventually took the plunge, albeit with some difficulty, to leave a world I was so passionate about and knew the contours of. Of course, shedding the CEO mantle was also a tough call. But that was how I joined the world of corporate communications.

After nineteen years of being in ITC, I believe what drew me to this role was the opportunity to learn business strategy in an ever-changing world, understand the perpetual value of brands, the nuances of marketing, the ability to shape and influence perceptions and drive impact. In retrospect, my journey underscores the importance of adaptability, conviction and the ability to engage and persuade—not from a position of authority, but through meaningful dialogue and shared purpose.

I have been told, and perhaps quite rightly, that the primary task of our function is to create, enhance and protect corporate reputation. To my mind, reputation is an outcome, and not the destination alone. I strongly believe that the primary task of corporate communications and PR is to enable an organisation in achieving extreme competitiveness.

The most important asset in a profession like ours is trust. People need to believe that what we say is honest and that our advice, views and actions are in their best interest. Whether it is among colleagues, leadership or external stakeholders, building trust is key.

Having spent nearly two decades at ITC, I can say that this journey into communications was not planned—it was a natural progression from my prior roles in public policy and economic development. The shift to corporate communications was less about changing fields and more about applying my experience in a new way — crafting communication strategies that can lend new wings to the competitiveness of the organisation, ensure effective implementation across a wide range of stakeholders and inspire teams that the best is yet to come.

# 5

# Sanjay Arora

## Former Head - Communications, Tata BlueScope Steel

~

*'What gets me to work every day is the joy of collaborating with my team, rolling up our sleeves and building something meaningful together.'*

I come from the beautiful valley town of Dehradun. Growing up there was a privilege. We were surrounded by nature and close-knit communities and had a strong sense of belonging. My father served in the DRDO, and my mother worked with ONGC.

I studied at St Joseph's Academy in Dehradun, a school that instilled discipline, values and a love for sports in me. I was always active in extracurricular activities and took on responsibilities from a young age. Life changed dramatically when I lost my father in an accident just after completing Class 12. While there was no financial pressure, the emotional and directional void was significant. I had to grow up quickly.

Coming from a defence background and living in the same city as the Indian Military Academy, I always dreamt of joining the Indian Army. But I chose not to pursue this given the circumstances. I graduated with a BCom from the DAV PG College in Dehradun.

Eventually, I mustered the courage to move to Mumbai and pursue an MBA in Marketing from the Institute for Technology and Management. I had no contacts in Mumbai, but the experience toughened me up. Hostel life, managing on my own and academic rigour shaped my early years.

My corporate journey began with Hughes Telecom (now Tata Teleservices) in sales. A chance meeting at Genesis PR changed my career's trajectory. While selling a phone line to Deepshikha Dharmaraj, she spotted potential in me and introduced me to public relations. That's how I began my career at Genesis as a junior associate. I was mentored by some fantastic professionals like Hina Huria, Girish Huria, Sandeep Dahiya and Kavita Rao over the next three years.

In 2003, I moved to Zee Telefilms, working closely with Ashish Kaulin, the corporate brand development team and handling content promotion for twenty-nine channels. I also played a key role during the ICC broadcast rights crisis. It was a fast-paced, demanding role that expanded my understanding of media and crisis communication.

In 2005, I joined Tata BlueScope Steel, a joint venture between Tata Steel and BlueScope Steel of Australia in Pune, as the head of communications. My nine years there were deeply formative. Tata taught me values, structure and process. I transitioned from corporate communications to marketing, and later, with the mentorship of MD Chetan Tolia, even explored business strategy as his executive assistant. This exposure gave me a 360-degree view of the business.

Craving more hands-on experience, I asked to lead sales and was posted as head of sales for the East region. I spent two enriching years across Jamshedpur and Kolkata. That phase taught me invaluable lessons in on-ground sales and customer engagement.

In 2011, I was brought in to head marketing and help build a retail business from scratch. I travelled extensively across India, setting up dealer and distributor networks. There are few parts of the country I have not visited by road, and this journey gave me a deep, grassroots understanding of India's markets and people.

After this stint, I went back to where I had started my journey. Genesis PR had become Genesis Burson Marsteller (now Burson India). I joined the firm in 2013 as managing partner, working closely with Vandana Sandhir and Nikhil Dey.

In about two years, I became the practice chair for corporate and financial clients. Heading a national role, I interacted with clients across the country, adapting my approach on the basis of the challenge.

In 2015, my wife Archana started Ants Digital and caught the digital wave at the right time. With good work and notable clients, she started building her own digital venture. Life was peaceful and both of us were very busy crafting good work for our respective clients.

In 2020, I decided it was time to move on and support Archana in scaling Ants Digital. It was a deeply emotional decision to leave Genesis, where I'd spent over a decade and the best years of my life. Transitioning from a stable corporate role to entrepreneurship, just as the pandemic hit, was not easy. But the desire to take on a new challenge outweighed the uncertainty.

I genuinely believe learning is a constant process—it does not come only from structured sources. You learn from your children, your colleagues, your family. Archana taught me about the digital space, and that helped me transition from traditional PR to a broader communication outlook. PR still remains very close to my heart.

As an entrepreneur, I have become more fearless. Being an employee means you're part of a system. But as an entrepreneur, the responsibility is different—you're accountable not just for yourself, but for the seventy-five others who depend on the organisation. From the smallest detail to the biggest strategic decision, it's all on you.

One of the campaigns I'm particularly proud of is the work we did for Bayer. It was a challenging mandate, managing communication across four internal teams while still aligning with the corporate narrative. Despite the complexities, we launched impactful campaigns like Better with Bayer and the '125 Years of Bayer' milestone campaign, both of which stand out as significant achievements.

Another fulfilling journey has been with a sixty-year-old finance company. When we started, digital adoption was minimal. Over two and a half years, we built immense trust in digital communication with their leadership team. Today, their marketing budgets prioritise digital—something I consider a big win. And of course, PR continues to be at the core of our work for them and many of our legacy clients.

I feel deeply satisfied with the path we are on. Of course, there's always more to achieve—that hunger never fades. What gets me to work every day is the joy of collaborating with my team, rolling up our sleeves and building something meaningful together.

# 6

# Melissa Arulappan

## DIRECTOR - COMMUNICATIONS, TARGET

*'I have been fortunate to have mentors throughout my career who have stood up for me and my team.'*

I WAS BORN IN BANGALORE, BUT MY HERITAGE IS A BLEND OF cultures—Mangalore from my mother's side and Chennai from my father's. My father worked with ITC, and my early years were defined by frequent relocations because of his job. We lived in Bangalore for the first four years of my life before moving to Munger, Bihar, where we stayed for two years. From there, we shifted to Chirala, a small village in Andhra Pradesh, where we spent five memorable years.

After five years in Chirala, we returned to Bangalore as my parents wanted better educational opportunities for my older sister, who was intellectually challenged. Back in Bangalore, I joined Sophia High School in sixth grade. It was there that another facet of my personality blossomed—my love for sports. After completing my schooling, I earned my bachelor's degree in Bangalore, excelling in both academics and sports, and graduating with a rank from Bangalore University. I then pursued my master's degree in Medical and Psychiatric Social Work at the Tata Institute of Social Sciences in Mumbai, winning the gold medal when I graduated.

Mumbai became a pivotal chapter in my life. I stayed there for six years, including my postgraduate studies, and began my professional journey in the city. During this time, I met my husband at university, and we eventually got married. However, as we wanted a better quality of life, Bangalore became the natural choice for us.

After my post-graduation, I took a part-time job for about six months with an NGO supported by the Ford Foundation. The focus was on identifying the needs of health-related NGOs, which gave me an initial glimpse into the world of CSR.

Not long after, I was headhunted by Glaxo for a very interesting role within their PR department, where CSR was integrated. At the time, I was twenty-three and was being trained to take over a role from an executive retiring the following year. It was an amazing learning experience and opportunity to step into such a significant role at a young age, especially when the average age of my department was more than double mine.

As part of the PR department, there was a prerequisite for me to have an education in public relations, and Glaxo sponsored my advanced PR diploma at the Xavier Institute of Communications (XIC). I worked at Glaxo for three years as executive—social work & public affairs, and I consider myself fortunate to have had Jane Swamy as my manager during my time there. During my time at Glaxo and soon after I graduated from XIC, Jane encouraged me to teach PR, and that's how my journey in teaching PR began, one that I continue even today.

In 1990, I moved to Bangalore and kept my options open to either continuing with CSR, my academic background, or pursue a full-time PR career. I ended up joining Corporate Voice Public Relations, which was then a division of the MAA Group, marking the official beginning of my PR consultancy journey. I was employee number two at Corporate Voice PR, where we started with just two clients.

I ended up staying at Corporate Voice for nineteen years. There was a lot of testing and learning and trial by fire, but I was also lucky that we had informal partnerships with international consultancies like Edelman, Manning, Selvage & Lee (MSL), Fleishman-Hillard and Weber Shandwick. I worked closely with all of them on several projects, building relationships, some of which I still maintain today. Eventually, we formalised our partnership with Weber Shandwick, and the company became Corporate Voice | Weber Shandwick and, after the merger, Weber Shandwick.

During my tenure, I became vice president, south and also headed learning and development for the company in India, which was an incredibly exciting and fulfilling role.

I gave myself two years to transition back into the corporate sector. I had not worked in the corporate world for nineteen years and was not sure how much had changed so the two years would help me ease myself back in. As a consultant, I worked like an in-house executive, providing strategic counsel and focusing on areas like media training and crisis communications workshops, while working with PR consultancies to execute campaigns. This break also gave me the flexibility to focus on passion projects, such as travelling and helping my daughter launch her charity bake sale.

After two years, I joined Quintiles, the US-based world leader in clinical research, where I worked for nine years. I was responsible for setting up their entire communications department in India. By the time I left, Quintiles had become a larger healthcare services firm IQVIA and grown to 18,000 people across the country, following a merger. In 2022, I joined Target to lead their communications department. The organisation's amazing culture was a big draw. I now lead a larger team, but the work continues to be exciting and very rewarding.

I have been fortunate to have mentors throughout my career who have stood up for me and my team. It is from them I have learnt to be equally fearless in taking decisions to ensure my teams are able to work with dignity and self-respect, even if that means giving up a client.

# 7

# Roma Balwani

### Former Chief Group Communications Officer, Mahindra

---

*'You have to find your place, be assertive and learn to be diplomatic.'*

I WAS BORN IN A POST-PARTITION HOUSEHOLD IN MUMBAI, then known as Bombay. I lived for twenty-three years of my life on the RP Masani Road, Matunga in Mumbai, popularly called Hollywood Lane, which had the likes of Prithviraj Kapoor's family and many more actors of that era as friendly neighbours. It was like living with an even larger family when you are doing namaste to every elder you meet.

I studied at the JB Vachha High School for Girls. I grew up as an awkward and shy back-bencher. I had a forward-looking mother as a role model. She was a math and science teacher in Sind, at a time when women were not allowed to work. For her my education was top priority. I was blessed with a soft-spoken father who was my spiritual guide. I could not have asked for more.

As in many households, with so many family members, I decided to work at the early age of seventeen, inexperienced but determined not to burden my parents and still pursue my education, along with my work.

In my spare time, I would visit a school for people with disabilities and learn about the challenges and how they coped with life. Life has come full circle, as I am now devoted to the cause of disability sport, especially for women who are specially-abled and talented in the sport of cricket despite the limitation of sound.

I studied at Jai Hind College. It was fun to begin with, but soon I wanted to do more in life, and switched to morning college, majored in economics and was lucky to be selected for a job with the engineering conglomerate L&T. It was my first nervous step into an unknown world, which had engineers, MBAs and the best-in-class processes for manufacturing.

As in every woman's life when she meets her life partner, marries, decides to raise a family, there comes a time to take the difficult decision of leaving one's job. Which I did with no regrets. During that time I took a break for six years. I was restless, and Mumbai is one city where you can try your hand at anything and actually succeed. I started working from home with a new career path as a creative consultant to advertising agencies.

I bounced back into my corporate career when my daughter was six years old. I joined an IT education company, Aptech, where I went back to a marketing job. Then came an opportunity when a sudden vacancy for a communications role came my way. My boss Ganesh Natarajan, the CEO, suggested I take up the role. In fact, wary of the profile, I told him I was too upfront and would not be able to do justice and I may not be able to handle journalists. He said to me, that is your strength, you are credible and you know the business.

He had more faith in me than I did in myself at that time. Today when I look back, that was probably the best decision I took.

As a family we moved cities due to my husband's transferrable job, soaked in the culture and cuisine of the states we lived in and made a diverse circle of friends. Each time I took up a job in a new city, it only helped me grow as a professional and widen my network. I call these colleagues my co-travellers.

We moved to Norway, when I was in a leadership role at Aptech. I had to resign and move to a business development consultancy role for the same company in a new country and in a new environment. I made it a point to assimilate with the local culture and people. We made some unforgettable and cherished memories there.

Through AIESEC, an international student body, which reached out to me in Oslo, I got the splendid opportunity to volunteer and help Indian students settle in Norway. Our home was always open for these students or young IT professionals, giving them tips and home-made dal chawal. It is probably the best example to me of reverse mentoring, as I learnt a lot from them.

A chance meeting during my stay in Oslo was with the then Indian ambassador to Norway, Gopalkrishna Gandhi, a renowned personality and the grandson of Mahatma Gandhi. I had started consulting as a communications director for an e-commerce company, eBookers. They wanted to offer travel products to Norwegians to visit India. I was also helping the consular office in reaching out to local trade bodies and helping in changing perceptions about Indian IT companies.

Back in India, after almost a three-year stint in the Nordic country, which helped me spread my network globally, I was fortunate to come back at a time when it was a thriving economy. I joined the Mahindra Group as their head of communications. I spent a glorious decade there, with exposure to a purpose-driven organisation. It was rebranding and repositioning its legacy brand at the time, and this was a unique opportunity to innovate in communications.

I joined Vedanta Group, a highly regulated global mining and oil company after that. Here we had to resurrect the brand and build the perception of a caring organisation.

Fate had some other plans for me. I was keen to give back to society, which had given me so much. I volunteered to be a pro-bono CEO of a non-profit, which is the governing body for deaf cricket in India, to help hearing-impaired cricketing talent to train and participate in national and international tournaments. My tenure with the Indian Deaf Cricket Association as CEO and brand custodian reflects a dedication to inclusivity in sports, where our team's collaborative efforts have amplified the platform for hearing-impaired athletes and secured global recognition for their talents. Recently I have started a new social enterprise as a co-founder of RB Foundation, which raises funds for the Indian Deaf Cricket Association and mentors non-profits for brand building.

My leadership focuses on fostering strategic partnerships and initiating programmes that resonate with our core values of empowerment and purpose-driven success.

# 8

# Rohit Bansal

GROUP HEAD - COMMUNICATIONS, RELIANCE INDUSTRIES LIMITED

---

*'Happenstance has played a pivotal role in my life.'*

I WAS BORN IN AGRA. MY FATHER WAS IN THE INDIAN FOREST Service and my mother a homemaker. Most of my childhood was spent in the forests of Uttar Pradesh (now Uttarakhand), in places like Gonda and Etawah. We had official elephants to help my father with his forest tours.

At some point, we moved to Mauritius. I attended two different schools during that time; one was Mahatma Gandhi Institute, a school gifted to Mauritius by India. After three years in Mauritius, we returned to Agra. Back in Agra, I attended a convent school and discovered tennis. Eventually, my parents decided that the unpredictability of Uttar Pradesh's political climate, which could affect my father's postings, was not ideal for my education. So, they made the decision to move me to a school in Delhi, setting the stage for the next chapter of my life. Many of my lifelong friends, some now remarkably successful, emerged from my time at Delhi Public School, RK Puram.

A defining moment of happenstance occurred later in life when I was a student at St Stephen's College. I entered a declamation contest at Lady Shri Ram College on Native American history—a topic I knew nothing about. With no preparation, I improvised and was rightly criticised.

As I waited at the bus stop outside, a stranger approached me. She praised my speaking skills but pointed out my lack of knowledge and suggested a career in journalism. She handed me a newspaper clipping—an ad from *The Times of India* seeking trainees to cover India's economic reforms. I rushed back, typed out an application and submitted it just after the deadline. Thankfully, the watchman let me in.

Though I was not initially shortlisted, Narayani Ganesh, a senior editor, later told me I had topped the test. She urged me to speak with the programme director, Vidyut Sarkar. He remembered me but said I had not been selected because I appeared indecisive as I was applying elsewhere too. I promised my commitment, and he added my name by hand. That decision changed my life.

Later, during interviews at *The Economic Times* and *The Times of India*, I stumbled again. My essay failed to impress the *ET* panel. But the *TOI* business editor asked if I could read a balance sheet. I said no, but I'd like to learn. He smiled and said, 'I'll put my faith in you.'

Those moments taught me to value serendipity, honesty and persistence. When I later worked at *The Financial Express*, my skill in simplifying complex topics, along with my fluency in Hindi and English, helped me connect with diverse audiences, both in print and on All India Radio.

I then moved from print to TV. I joined Television 18 for the wrong reason—essentially to double my salary. It was an enticing prospect to have twice the disposable income. But in television, I learnt the fundamentals of the medium—things like the placement of the camera, where you sit and how crucial audio is. If the audio is off, even the best visuals will not matter.

Serendipity struck again when I became disillusioned by the lack of audience for TV18's venture. They lacked any significant distribution. So, I switched to Zee TV, which was thriving in the entertainment space. They had a twenty-minute news bulletin, Zee News, airing at 10 p.m., during prime time. It was a big hit and led by Rajat Sharma. After he interviewed me, things went well, and he proposed that we expand the bulletin by ten minutes, adding a segment we could call Zee Business. He asked if I would come on board to help with the expansion, alongwith my colleague, Rakesh Khar.

Having worked at *ET* and *TOI*, both of us were used to large audiences. But in TV18, we had struggled to gather any audience. We decided to take the plunge and join Zee TV, but just as we were about to join, Rajat Sharma and Subhash Chandra, the chairman, had a very public falling out. Rajat Sharma walked out of Zee TV, taking around thirty to forty reporters with him. The situation seemed dire, as we thought it was going to be the end of the road for us.

But then, out of the blue, I received a call from the CEO of Zee News. He said their chairman wanted to meet me. I was surprised—how had they found out about me? It turned out that they had found my CV and notes on Rajat Sharma's desk, so they decided to reach out and see if I was still available.

The best part was that the channel was in Hindi, so I had to put my rusty Hindi to the test. I had to communicate in a way that made sense on TV, which was a challenge, but was also an opportunity to grow. I also had to assemble a team that spoke Hindi fluently. While some content was still in English, Hindi was strongly encouraged. What helped me thrive there was my ability to connect and communicate in a language other than English. This skill became crucial for my future role at AIR. Happenstance and multi-skilling never worked against me.

Even though I was not formally trained in economics past Class 12, I became a business editor at Zee when I was in my early thirties. Soon after, I became the resident editor of *The Financial Express*, just after Zee. I was thirty-one or thirty-two when I transitioned to *The Financial Express*, a paper that ranked number two after *The Economic Times* in IRS figures at the time. It was an incredible honour, and the challenge was immense.

So, I threw myself into the trenches—reporting, editing, even understanding how the paper was printed. I worked like a manager some days and like a reporter on others. This hands-on experience helped me build credibility in the newsroom.

Then, one day Rajat Sharma called me. We met late at night, after I had finished my work at *The Financial Express*. We had dinner, talked till early in the morning, and then, as he dropped me to my car, I finally asked him, 'I think you called me for something, but you haven't said it yet.' That's when he said, 'Yes, I want you to work with me.' I had been waiting for that moment, for an opportunity to exit *The Financial Express* if the right offer came along.

I did not try to out-negotiate him. I told him, 'I can't out-negotiate you. You're Rajat Sharma. So, it's best you send me an email with your offer, and I'll decide if I want to take it.' He did, and it was an offer I could not refuse. More than the financial terms, I felt they were kind to me. Rajat Sharma and his wife, Ritu Dhawan, treated me like family, ensuring we ate together, thought together and struggled together despite limited resources.

This sense of loyalty and unity felt different from my time at TV18, where Raghav's leadership was more inclusive of outsiders. But at India TV, the tight-knit family atmosphere, particularly in the Hindi world, struck a chord with me. I rose to become the chief operating officer, and soon enough, investments started to come in, improving our situation.

At some point, I saved enough money to attend the Harvard Business School for an Advanced Management Program (AMP), which cost $60,000 at the time. The dollar was not as high as it is now, so it was more affordable. Instead of spending on a car or other luxuries, I chose to invest on myself. The AM programme made me reflect deeply on the future of television, print and digital media. I did not want to just keep hopping from job to job—I wanted to think strategically. But what I ended up doing for the next five years was consulting, in a joint venture with Hammurabi-Solomon.

My college roommate, Prabir Jha, who is now a major figure in the HR space, reached out in 2014. At the time, he was heading HR at Reliance Industries. He was looking for candidates to help build the company's reputation. I sent him the names of a few friends, but they did not quite click. Frustrated, I asked him what he was really looking for. He replied, 'I want you.' I laughed and said, 'Why didn't you just say that?'

I went to Mumbai, where Prabir had paid for my flight and hotel.. When I arrived, he looked at me and remarked, 'Aren't you a little overdressed to meet Mukesh Ambani?' I had not realised I was going to meet him. I had just dressed like I would for any professional meeting. But this was different. So, we went to a small room on the floor where Mukesh bhai sat.

When Mukesh bhai walked in, he immediately took my hand, sat down and spoke for eight minutes straight. What he shared was privileged information, and it seemed like a done deal. Apparently, Prabir had given him a pre-read, and Mukesh bhai was well-prepared. He laid out what he expected, and before I knew it, he assumed I would start the next day.

Meanwhile, I kept thinking about my wife, who was in Noida, and what her reaction would be. I hesitated to ask her, unsure if she would think this was a bad move. Finally, I called her, nervous about her response. To my surprise, she said, 'They're a great company, and they even have a hospital. So, as long as my parents are around, you should work with them.' It was a moment of clarity for me, as she was thinking pragmatically about the future.

So, that's how I ended up at Reliance. I was warned that it would be a tough assignment, with people at my level not lasting long. But I adopted a 'first-day mindset', and that approach has remained with me for the past eleven years. I focus on what I need to do now rather than rest on past achievements.

When Jio was launched in front of me, I had to constantly remind myself of my humble beginnings as a reporter and special correspondent. Here I was, sitting alongside Deepak Parekh from HDFC, Adil Zainulbhai from McKinsey and Nirupa Rao, former foreign secretary and ambassador. I contributed in my own way, but it took thorough preparation to be of real assistance.

Where else would I get this perspective, other than at Reliance? When challenges arise, I do not view them solely as PR or media issues. I approach them through the lens of what I learnt in the AMP at Harvard: running a business and managing reputational risk, which starts at the very top. Mitigating risks does not solely fall on the communications teams, as some might think.

I approach issues from a CEO's point of view, considering what impacts the brand's value or poses a danger to it. Communications professionals are essential, but they are an extension of the CEO's broader strategy—they're not the ones who can solve everything on their own.

These years at Reliance have been a unique blend of experiences, combining the mindset of a start-up with that of a seasoned professional. It has been about learning, adapting and applying these varied lessons to create meaningful impact.

# 9

# Sudeep Bhalla

## Head - Corporate Communications, Tata Motors

---

*'We need to harmonise AI with EQ to deliver purposeful communication.'*

I WAS BORN IN MUMBAI IN A HOUSEHOLD ROOTED IN academia. My father taught advanced mathematics to postgraduates at the Bhabha Atomic Research Centre. My mother dedicated herself to our home, while my elder sister chose to become an engineer. The environment I grew up in valued STEM (science, technology, engineering and mathematics) and anything else was not considered worthy. But I found my calling elsewhere. I was fortunate to stumble, discover and continue to chart long miles on the ever-adventurous trek of public relations.

Encouraged to pursue engineering, I had enrolled for it following my secondary education. However, I soon realised that this discipline did not resonate with my aspirations. Making a pivotal decision to withdraw, I opted instead to complete my graduation via a correspondence programme, studying English and economics. Simultaneously, I took up a job to gain some work experience. The three years spent doing this were then perceived as unproductive, but instilled in me valuable life lessons. They equipped me with the confidence to take my own decisions, question the set norms and go against them when needed.

Being interested in marketing and communications, I pursued an MBA programme after my graduation where I serendipitously discovered the field of PR through a book in the institute's library. And though it offered only a cursory overview, it ignited my curiosity. Fortuitously, a classmate's sibling worked at a leading PR firm and, at my request, supported my candidature for an internship there. This exposure to the real world of PR in the summer of 1995, its intricacies, dos and don'ts, engagements with clients and media, planning and messaging set me on a path from which I have never looked back.

I have been privileged to work for a meaningful duration with three prominent PR consulting firms. Beginning my career at Corporate Voice, I transitioned to Genesis and later to IPAN. While my role at the first two firms was broadly client servicing and business development, I joined the third for an entrepreneurial opportunity—to launch the news distribution services of *BusinessWire* in India. In between, I also had the opportunity to venture into investor relations consulting with Thomson Financial, a stint cut short in the aftermath of the global economic meltdown that followed the gruesome 9/11 attacks.

After working for nearly a decade on the advisory side, I shifted focus to corporate communications, joining Yes Bank for just few months, and then Citibank in 2004. Overnight, I had jumped from arguably the world's smallest bank to the world's largest bank! From Citi I moved to DBS Bank to lead their communications, marketing and CSR, exploring and adding new skills and dimensions, that were previously uncharted.

My relentless pursuit for growth led me to explore the dynamic domain of telecom with Vodafone as my destination in 2012. After nearly an eight-year stint marked by several award-winning campaigns and exhilarating challenges, including a gory public battle fought for the survival of the organisation, I decided to explore again, and this time, transitioned from mobile to mobility!

I joined Tata Motors just as the world had shut down in its attempt to control the pandemic of COVID-19. Notably, April 2020, my first month, gained the dubious distinction of being the only month in the history of the Indian automobile industry to record zero vehicle sales, as all dealer showrooms stayed shut adhering to the strict COVID-19 protocols. Despite such an extraordinary beginning, my tenure here has been incredibly enriching.

Joining Tata Motors introduced me to a new world of multiple firsts—working for an Indian company in the manufacturing sector, exposure to blue-collar workforce and unions and, most importantly, the onus of building on the rich legacy I now had the honour of being a part of. Being a global 44-billion-dollar enterprise, the sheer scale and diversity of the assignments that I have had the privilege of associating with is unparalleled. From launch to expo, merger and demerger, acquisition and sell-off, listing and delisting, I continue to be a part of several strategic initiatives.

Over the years, I have also had the opportunity to grow as a leader. Preferring empowerment over oversight, I like to foster an environment where team members take a bold approach and question the status quo. I implicitly trust my colleagues, always urging them to extend their intellectual boundaries and gain new experiences. My biggest achievement till date, I believe, is to have three of my former team members successfully lead the communication function of their respective organisations. Each of these organisations is large and a leader in their respective industry vertical and is publicly listed.

To conclude, as I reflect on my diverse academic and career path, I recognise that each twist and turn has not only shaped my personal and professional identity but has also reinforced the importance of adaptability and lifelong learning. Today, as we stand at the intersection of traditional PR with the emerging digital landscape, I am excited about the future possibilities. The integration of artificial intelligence in communication not only presents opportunities for enhanced efficiency but also invites us to rethink the very essence of how we connect with audiences. My motivation now is to not just respond to these changes but lead them.

And as we navigate this ever-evolving landscape, we must make communication not just impactful but also deeply human — one that values authenticity, purpose and the power of storytelling. An eternal optimist, I'm hopeful that together as the PR fraternity, we can redefine the narrative, shaping a world where communication transcends mere information and truly resonates with every human being.

# 10

# Ophira Bhatia

### Vice President, India & Lead, AMEA - Corporate & Government Affairs, Mondelez International

---

*'The most valuable part of my journey has always been the people ... The relationships I have built have been at the heart of my career.'*

I'M A BOMBAY GIRL, BORN AND RAISED IN THIS VIBRANT CITY. My father was a businessman, and my mother was a homemaker who skilfully managed our bustling household of six with me being the youngest of four.

My journey into public relations was serendipitous. After completing my schooling at Hill Grange High School, I went on to earn a degree in economics from St Xavier's College. It was there that one of the counsellors recognised my knack for communication. She encouraged me to pursue a social communications course at Sophia College. I had a dream of working in advertising, so in a way it all worked out.

I fulfilled that dream with an internship at Chaitra Leo Burnett, which gave me four amazing months of working in a field I was most curious about. While my daily tasks were mundane like logging tapes, the experience at Chaitra Leo Burnett was anything but that. It introduced me to the vibrant, high-energy and creative world of advertising. One campaign that stood out was the launch of Thums Up cans in 1996–97. As a newcomer, it was thrilling to witness, especially the unforgettable stunt of a young man jumping off a cliff to promote the product. I even kept the first can we received at the agency as a cherished keepsake.

After that internship, I discovered that client servicing roles in advertising required an MBA and realised I would need to work more to gain a deeper understanding of the industry. However, around this time, a chance meeting with Roger Pereira (an advertising veteran) completely altered the direction of my career. After a great conversation, as I was about to leave, he asked if I'd consider joining him. Roger, who introduced me to the world of PR, had just launched one of India's first PR firms—Roger Pereira Communications (R&PM). I agreed, and that decision shaped the next sixteen years of my life.

There was no looking back after that. My work at Roger Pereira Communications was both fulfilling and challenging, offering me opportunities to grow and learn. One of my first major campaigns was the launch of Otis elevators.

As I moved up the ranks at Roger Pereira Communications, I had the privilege of working alongside brilliant minds like the late Allwyn Fernandes (former journalist at *The Times of India*), Ashoke Bijapurkar (leading advertising professional) and, of course, Roger Pereira himself. I managed major accounts across industries such as Visa, General Electric and

TCS, among others. I also had the opportunity to work with several Tata companies and engage in pro bono projects, which introduced me to a deeply rewarding and impactful side of the work.

We did PR very differently in those days—at R&PM we called it 'reputation management', since it was beyond media relations to overall stakeholder management. This included conceptualising white papers, representations on behalf of our clients to external stakeholders (including the government), creative work (yes, we had a department in those days), knowledge management for our clients and many diverse experiences beyond media.

In those early days, I learnt the importance of staying informed. To serve clients effectively, it was not enough to just understand their business. One also needed a strong grasp of what was happening in the world. I remember combing through newspapers every morning. It felt tedious at the time, but this habit helped me lay the foundation for a robust understanding of the industry and made me a trusted consultant to clients. During those years, we also had tie-ups with international consultancies like Burson Marsteller and then Edelman, where we were provided international training and insights that exposed me to global ways of doing business.

After sixteen years in one firm (when I left, I was the corporate practice head and lead of the Mumbai office), I made the jump to the corporate side when Cadbury, approached me to join their team. Transitioning from a consultancy professional to an in-house role marked a significant shift in my career, but it's a decision I am glad I made. It provided me with a fresh perspective on reputation management and PR while also allowing me to be part of the leadership team of a large business in India. My learnings, experiences and work have transformed me from a PR specialist to a corporate affairs professional. It also taught me the value of recognising that every decision I make for the business, I make as a leader of the business.

I have been at Cadbury, now Mondelez International, for over thirteen years. During this time, I witnessed the company's transformation along with my own as my role expanded beyond India to cover the entire region—Asia Pacific, Middle East and Africa. Overseeing six business units across thirteen time zones, with each market presenting its own set of challenges—it's this diversity that keeps me motivated and excited every day.

I have often been told that one of my strengths is my ability to take a step back and view things from a broader perspective without losing sight of the finer details. Another defining trait of mine is resilience. I have had my share of setbacks—whether in client relationships, challenging projects or other aspects of work. While no career is without its obstacles, what sets me apart is my ability to bounce back, learn from those experiences and keep moving forward.

Loyalty is another value I cherish. Whether it's for a company, a project or my team, I am deeply committed to seeing things through. This sense of dedication is something I bring to every aspect of my work. In essence, attention to detail, resilience and loyalty are the qualities that truly define me.

To younger professionals in the field of PR, my biggest advice is to value consistency. Over my career, I have been committed to only two companies, dedicating significant time to each. In today's fast-paced world, it's common for people with just a few years of experience to switch jobs multiple times. But I believe staying in a role for a significant period—

at least five to six years—allows one to truly learn, grow and mature in their career. It's not about staying stagnant but about giving yourself the time to build depth and expertise.

For me, the most valuable part of my journey has always been the people. Whether it was working with Roger, Allwyn, Ashoke or my leaders and team members at Mondelez (my functional leaders like Jin Montesano, Janice Armstrong and Russ Dyer and business leaders like Anand Kripalu, Manu Anand, Chandramouli V. and Deepak Iyer), the relationships I have built have been at the heart of my career. Many team members have been with me for eight to twelve years, a testament to the passion and excitement we share for our work.

Instilling that passion is something I take seriously as a leader. If you're not genuinely excited about your work, it's hard to find fulfilment—and that's when the temptation to jump ship arises. Passion is infectious, and I have always strived to infuse that energy into my leadership style.

Reflecting on my thirty-year journey, all I can say is that it's been immensely rewarding. I have been fortunate to work with two remarkable organisations that allowed me to continuously learn and grow with every new challenge. It's been an incredible journey, and I'm excited to keep evolving in this ever-changing field.

# 11

# Nandini Chatterjee

FORMER CHIEF MARKETING & COMMUNICATIONS OFFICER, PwC INDIA

*'Be practical, stay stakeholder-focused and keep experimenting.'*

I WAS BORN IN AMBALA, WHERE MY FATHER WAS POSTED AS A doctor in the army. Being part of the armed forces meant we moved frequently across the country—from Ambala to Jhansi, Guwahati, Babina, Allahabad, Varanasi, Ahmednagar, Amritsar and finally to Delhi after my father retired. In just ten years, I must have changed around eight schools. While constantly moving could be seen as disruptive, it actually gave me invaluable experiences.

At each location, I typically attended convent schools, which often reserved seats for army children. I studied at St Francis in Jhansi, St John's in Varanasi and St Mary's in Guwahati, among others. These schools offered a sense of familiarity even in unfamiliar places. Later, in Amritsar, I joined Kendriya Vidyalaya for Class 9 and 10 as the nearest convent school was too far from the cantonment. It turned out to be a great decision. After Amritsar, we moved to Delhi, where I joined DPS Mathura Road for Class 11 and 12.

Post school, I pursued a BCom at Lady Shri Ram College (LSR). After LSR, I went on to do my post-graduation in international trade from the Department of Business Management at Punjab University, Chandigarh.

After completing my master's, I started working at Hotline TV in the product management team. It was not through campus placement—I had done my summer training with Ballarpur Industries and made some connections that helped me apply. At Hotline TV, I was involved in everything from advertising to in-store branding, outdoor campaigns, research and overall product management.

A highlight from that time was attending a presentation by Alyque Padamsee from Lintas. It was for a television and appliances campaign, and hearing him present was incredibly inspiring. Later, my managers at Hotline TV sent me to Lintas for two months of hands-on training. They believed it was important for me to understand not just the theory, but the ground-level execution.

I began by working across diverse sectors—steel, infrastructure, chemicals, television and electronics—gaining a broad base of experience. During my time at Jindal Steel (JSPL), I gradually started moving towards communications. It was at DuPont, where I managed corporate affairs, that my focus on media and communications really started taking shape.

Unlike many in communications today who come from journalism or consultancy backgrounds, my path was different. But looking back, I think what helped me was my deep understanding of how brands are built—from marketing to consumer insights to storytelling and messaging. I learnt how to structure narratives that resonate, and that foundation has stayed with me.

That experience instilled in me a deep appreciation for the value of research and its role in shaping effective communication. It helped me develop a habit of always viewing things from the lens of the consumer, the user or the stakeholder—keeping their perspective at the centre. Over time, this approach shaped how I thought about communication: always with a larger purpose and clear objective. Whether it was messaging, narrative, execution or measurement, I believed each element should align seamlessly with that core purpose.

But it was at PwC from 2003 onwards where my journey in corporate communications came to bloom fully. Over twenty-one years, I built and led communication strategies that evolved with the times—introducing digital marketing, building in-house creative and video teams and emphasising internal communication as a cornerstone of reputation management. These were years of experimentation, trust and impact, where I was given the space to think like an entrepreneur within a global brand. I was able to introduce ideas and innovations based on what I anticipated the future would demand.

My approach was simple: be practical, stay stakeholder-focused and keep experimenting. If something worked, we scaled it. If it did not, we moved on. And along the way, we kept building relationships—with stakeholders, media, partners and internal teams.

In total, I bring over thirty-five years of professional experience, with the first two decades in product management and marketing roles, and the latter in strategic communications.

Today, I work with different companies in a consulting capacity. I work as a strategic advisor to Shree Cement, helping build their corporate brand and reputation.

Overall, it's been a rich and fulfilling journey—rooted in product, mature in communication and always driven by purpose and passion.

# 12

# Paresh Chaudhry

### FORMER GROUP PRESIDENT & GLOBAL BRAND CUSTODIAN, ADANI GROUP

---

*'Be transparent, acknowledge challenges and share a clear vision for the future. That is what builds credibility.'*

I HAIL FROM A SIMPLE MIDDLE-CLASS FAMILY AND WAS RAISED in Bandra East, Mumbai. My father, a strikingly handsome Thakur from a township in Uttar Pradesh, ran away from his village with dreams of becoming a Bollywood star. He spent a few years acting in films before eventually giving up on that dream. My mother, a die-hard Maharashtrian, came from a family deeply rooted in journalism.

I graduated from National College in Bandra, Mumbai, after attending St Anne's High School in Pali Hill. Bandra East was different back then. I grew up in an MIG colony run by MHADA. My father secured our home through the lottery system, borrowing the initial deposit of ₹300–400.

I played a lot of cricket and was selected for the under-nineteen team. My father told me that he could not afford proper shoes for me to practise. My mother explained our middle-class reality and the risks involved. Despite my passion, I had to choose between studying hard or committing fully to cricket. Given our circumstances, I chose to focus on my studies and support my family.

An unexpected hurdle arose after my graduation when University of Bombay professors went on strike, delaying our results. I missed the application deadline for MMS (MBA) programmes in Mumbai, including my top choice, JBIMS. Back then, SP Jain and NMIMS were not as popular, and Bajaj was the gold standard. With limited options, I consulted my family friend again, who suggested a Pune University MBA (PUMBA). I completed my MBA and excelled. I learnt engagement nuances, working with external faculty, recruitment and corporate clients. I visited companies, often hearing, 'Who goes to the University of Pune? We only go to FMS, IIMs, or Bajaj.' It was then that I promised myself to engage with any college that reached out for guest lectures, top-tier or not, and share my knowledge. I have kept that promise to this day.

After my MBA, I joined HTA (Hindustan Thompson Associates) and worked on the launch of Hero Honda's first self-start bike. The campaign included on-ground activation, radio and print flyers. However, I soon realised that advertising was not for me—late starts, endless coffee breaks and brainstorming sessions that often led to social drinking. It was not the environment I enjoyed working in. In contrast, I saw my father at Siemens having a disciplined routine.

Then came an opportunity at Raymond, the most aspirational clothing brand at the time. There were 6,000 applicants for only four vacancies. After a gruelling selection process, I made it, competing against candidates from IIMs and JBIMS. It was one of the happiest days for my parents. My father, who felt guilty about the end of my cricket dream, was thrilled. The role had rigour, discipline and a clear path forward. I would become an area sales manager (ASM), which came with a second-hand company car, a Fiat. At the time, my father did not even own a scooter.

Six months later, I finally got market exposure and saw how sales operated—distributor relations, fabric allocations and perks for wholesalers. It was not the marketing I had envisioned when starting out. I started looking elsewhere. That's when I met Habil Khorakiwala of Wockhardt. A conversation led to an interview, and within twenty-four hours, I had an offer. I left Raymond. At Wockhardt, I finally got into marketing and began in product management. I was handling anti-infectives when a bigger opportunity arose—launching India's first corporate hospital, Wockhardt Hospitals in Bangalore.

That marked the start of my journey in consumer engagement. During this period, I truly understood the importance of consumer behaviour. Beyond medical expertise, people sought compassion. This principle applies to all areas—marketing, sales, communications or PR. Putting yourself in others' shoes helps craft better strategies and achieve meaningful goals. This realisation shaped my journey.

Later, Khorakiwala called me to Mumbai to manage a 400-bed hospital, now under Fortis. I transitioned from marketing head to COO. We were expanding, planning four hospitals across Mumbai. Despite the career prospects, I had built a life in Bangalore with strong community ties, friendships and involvement in Round Table India. So, I made a bold decision—I quit.

In 1996, I joined SmithKline Beecham as a group product manager, handling anti-infectives and launching India's first hepatitis A and B vaccines. My crisis management experience led me to corporate communications, despite the lack of a formal PR function. I instinctively handled media relations, major announcements and internal crises. A major IR issue at SmithKline caught global attention, prompting the head of communications to fly in from London. Impressed by my approach, he took me to the UK for three months of intensive training in media and corporate communications.

That experience solidified my transition into corporate communications. I formalised PR and internal communication frameworks for SmithKline Beecham in India. I also introduced employee volunteering programmes, encouraging the staff to engage with the Society for Spastic Children.

That period marked the start of my journey in communications and CSR, deepening my understanding of internal communication. After four years at SmithKline Beecham, Mr Brar invited me to join Ranbaxy in January 2000 and move to Delhi from Bangalore—something I initially resisted but eventually embraced. Ranbaxy was an incredible experience. In a global role, I established communication strategies worldwide. One of my key contributions was taking the Ranbaxy brand to North America.

One key principle I have always upheld is authenticity. I have always advised my teams and leaders: never lie. Be transparent, acknowledge challenges and share a clear vision for the future. That is what builds credibility.

Ranbaxy was a fantastic chapter, but my dream company came next. One day, Vindi Banga, then chairman of Hindustan Lever, called me. With my ageing parents and being years away from Mumbai, I was ready to return. Vindi asked if I wanted to join Levers, and I replied, 'Tomorrow morning.'

When I joined Hindustan Lever (then HLL), the company's focus was exclusively on corporate affairs and policy management. It was one of my best jobs. Then, Mukesh Ambani started calling. Initially, I had no intention of leaving. For over a year, he engaged with me, always with the permission of my chairman and HR head. I had to formally notify them every time I met him, ensuring transparency. Eventually, I could not say no.

My move from Unilever to Reliance was not for financial reasons—I had a fulfilling life at Unilever, making a meaningful impact daily. But when Mukesh Ambani said he needed to build a strong corporate reputation, I saw the chance to create something transformative. That hunger for impact has always driven me.

One defining trait of Mukesh Ambani, much like Gautam Adani, who I worked with later, is his unwavering belief in India's reform and nation-building.

I spent close to four years at Reliance, building the corporate communications team from scratch. Before my arrival, communications was a secondary function managed by HR or finance. They needed a dedicated leader to establish a global communications framework, and I took on that challenge.

Leaving my role as group president of communications was a tough decision. One of my lasting contributions at Reliance was developing a crisis management manual that became an industry benchmark, adopted by the Indian Chamber of Commerce (ICC). After leaving Reliance, Sam Balsara approached me to join Madison, marking my first formal engagement with a PR consultancy. Until then, I had relied on in-house teams, only bringing in PR firms for specific projects like launching Reliance Retail or managing Mumbai Indians.

I knew Sam from industry panels. He was a sharp leader, and Madison was well-established, though their PR wing was struggling. The company was looking for a leader for two to three years and needed a turnaround. Sam told me, 'You come in, build the team, and I'll invest in PR. I'll even give you equity.' That challenge excited me.

I spent five great years at Madison before the next move. Around 2011–12, Gautam Adani approached me. After Reliance, I felt I needed a break before another big corporate role. Moving from Reliance to Madison was a significant shift, and now from Ambani to Adani was another.

At Adani Group, managing crises was a key feature of my role. When I started, the team had fifty members. I scaled it up to 300 over four years, a demanding but fulfilling task.

This journey—balancing professional growth with personal responsibilities—has been demanding, but it has also been deeply rewarding.

# 13

# Paroma Roy Chowdhury

### FORMER CHIEF COMMUNICATIONS & PUBLIC AFFAIRS OFFICER, DREAM SPORTS

*'I have learnt that resilience is the cornerstone of career success. No matter what the setbacks are, you have to pick yourself up, dust off and move forward.'*

I GREW UP IN KOLKATA IN A HIGHLY EDUCATED BENGALI family with modest means. Academics were central to our lives—my mother was a college professor, my father a bureaucrat and most of my relatives were in academia. My schooling, inspired by Tagore's Shantiniketan, emphasised character building, art, culture and literature over conventional studies, fostering my lifelong love for books, theatre and art films.

Despite the school's unconventional approach, I excelled academically, consistently ranking at the top of my class. My parents, though encouraging, placed immense pressure to excel, which I managed by maintaining good grades. Outside academics, my childhood was multifaceted—I learnt classical dance, attended art school, performed theatre and started writing.

After high school, I shifted to a girls' school known for its academic rigour and later joined Presidency College for pure humanities, bypassing science. Writing became a source of pocket money during college, and I contributed extensively to *The Telegraph*. Alongside academics, I remained deeply involved in dance and other creative pursuits. Growing up in a family with strong feminist role models, I developed a deep sense of independence and outspokenness.

With a scholarship and top grades in both my bachelor's and master's, I initially considered a PhD in international relations but gravitated towards journalism. After a chance encounter at *Business Standard*, I secured my first job despite having no background in business reporting. It was a steep learning curve, but I gained valuable experience in editing and reporting.

At twenty-three, I married and moved to Mumbai, where *Business Standard* transferred me. I balanced the demands of reporting and motherhood, transitioning to feature writing to accommodate my growing family. After four years there, I joined *The Economic Times*, helping launch the Corporate Dossier section, which was an incredible learning experience.

Later on, I was transferred to Delhi *ET*, but I disliked it immediately. It lacked the lively, vibrant vibe of Bombay and just did not feel cool at all. Despite my initial dislike, I worked there for a year, managing both Corporate Dossier and Brand Equity from Delhi. Then I made a big mistake—I moved to *Business Today*. I was heavily wooed into the role, but it turned out to be a poor fit. I just could not adapt to the magazine space, which was very different from what I was used to.

Around this time, I was awarded a prestigious journalism fellowship at Cambridge—competitive, with only six winners globally. I stayed for a few months longer than planned, immersing myself in an incredible experience. My dissertation was on the glass ceiling, comparing India and the UK. One professor even encouraged me to pursue a PhD, offering a research grant, but I had to decline because my son was very young, and balancing that with my husband's career was challenging.

After Cambridge, I returned to *Business Today*, feeling increasingly dissatisfied. My internship at the *Financial Times* had shown me what truly excellent journalism looked like, and I realised I could not continue in a role that no longer inspired me.

That's when life took a serendipitous turn. In 2001, ISB was starting, and I was recommended for their start-up team by Sumantra Ghoshal, whom I had interviewed during my time at *ET*. The role had nothing to do with PR, but it was one of the best years of my life. Building something on that scale—collaborating with Harvard, Wharton, LBS and McKinsey—was extraordinary. However, managing family commitments while shuttling between Hyderabad and Delhi every week proved unsustainable after a year.

Next, I joined GE Capital, thanks to a chance encounter with Tiger Tyagarajan, who recommended me. GE was intense, with one of the toughest bosses I have ever worked for, but I learnt invaluable lessons in execution, responsibility and business writing. After four years, I left because GE's focus shifted towards outsourcing, which did not appeal to me.

A short stint at Hewlett-Packard followed, but I did not enjoy it due to its rigid decision-making process. Then came Airtel, a fascinating yet highly complex environment during the telecom boom. I spent three challenging but rewarding years there, learning to handle scale and crises.

In 2007, I was headhunted by Google for a major role. The seven years I spent there were some of the best of my career, working with a global team and putting India on the map for Google. However, by the end, I was bored and unwilling to relocate to Singapore or the US due to family commitments.

When Nikesh Arora, whom I had worked with at Google, moved to SoftBank, he invited me to join him. It was a major, global role with exciting challenges, but after a year, Nikesh left, and I stayed on, managing complex projects. By 2020, SoftBank shifted focus, and my role would have significantly downsized. It felt like the right time to move on.

Then came a brief but insightful stint at Dream11, where I worked on policy communication. Though I did not connect with the gaming industry, the experience taught me a lot about navigating regulatory challenges.

I was on the verge of joining a multinational bank when Byju Raveendran of Byju's, then the largest edtech company in the world valued at ₹22 billion, himself reached out to me. Byju, ever the charmer, has an undeniable ability to win people over. It was an opportunity that seemed too good to pass up—but in hindsight, it turned out to be the biggest mistake of my career.

At the time, though, it felt like the right choice. They were the largest start-up, with grand plans for an IPO. I spent twelve challenging months there before managing to leave in May 2023. After leaving, I took a much-needed break.

Between May and December, I decided not to work in a conventional sense. However, I kept myself engaged by teaching a MBA course at Shiv Nadar University, focusing on storytelling and personal brand—a fulfilling pursuit. Around this time, I began a conversation with Pramath Sinha, the chairman of Ashoka University's board of trustees, and my erstwhile boss at ISB, who needed some assistance. I joined Ashoka as an advisor, working closely with the board and the vice chancellor. This role allows me to contribute without handling day-to-day operations, which I opted out of by design.

In my career, I have been fortunate to work on transformative campaigns and roles. From honing business communication at GE to scaling crisis management at Airtel and putting Google India on the map, each stint taught me something invaluable. At SoftBank, I had the unique challenge of establishing its presence in India, even taking on an Asia-wide role. Dream11 was another milestone, marking my first experience with a real start-up. Though my time at Byju's was a misstep, it came from a place of ambition—I believed in their vision. I now prioritise projects that align with my personal and professional values. I continue to take on special projects, like partnerships for Ashoka and initiatives with literary and cultural events such as the Kolkata Literary Meet. These allow me to blend my passion for creativity with impactful work.

Looking ahead, I'm content with the freedom to choose how I contribute. Whether it's writing, consulting or pursuing my love for art and theatre, I'm committed to making the most of my time. After more than three decades in journalism and corporate roles, I have earned the privilege to focus on what truly matters to me—flexibility, meaningful work and personal growth. I have learnt that resilience is the cornerstone of career success. No matter what the setbacks are, you have to pick yourself up, dust off and move forward. Throughout my journey, I remain true to my passions for writing and storytelling, supported by a foundation of resilience, creativity and a strong sense of self.

# 14

# Madhu Chhibber

EVP & Head - Corporate Communications, HDFC Bank

―⁂―

*'My journey has been rooted in strong personal values, love of communication and hunger for knowledge.'*

IF I WERE TO DESCRIBE MY PROFESSIONAL JOURNEY IN TWO words, they would be, 'unscripted' and 'fulfilling'. Nothing about my career—from the profession I entered, to the cities I have lived and worked in—was premeditated. Public relations was not on my radar. In fact, it was not even on the list of career options that I was considering and the reason was probably because I did not know much about it. And yet, through a serendipitous meeting with a prominent name in the communications fraternity, I found myself joining a profession that has given me the opportunity to shape narratives that matter.

I was born in Pune, Maharashtra, and raised in various towns and cities across the country, which exposed me to India's rich cultural diversity. My father served in the Indian

Army with distinction, and my mother was a homemaker. From my father, I inherited not just a love for the country but a deep-rooted value system based on integrity, discipline and commitment. My mother played a formative role in shaping the woman I became. A homemaker for much of my growing up years, she gradually allowed herself to pursue work once my sister and I were in middle school and less dependent on her. Deeply artistic, with a refined eye for detail, she worked as interior designer for a leading luxury hotel chain, leaving her signature on some of their most elegant spaces.

In Class 8, we moved to Delhi, which became the base for my education and, eventually, my early professional life. My paternal grandfather and father passed on to me an enduring love of news—almost addictive in its pull. The newspaper was sacred; news on radio Vividh Bharati was a must. Current affairs were dinner table conversations. This early immersion in discussions about events in the world around me perhaps planted the first seeds of interest in communication and shaping narratives, even if I did not recognise it at the time.

I enjoyed my studies, though I would not call myself studious in the conventional sense. A commerce graduate, I also earned a BEd degree, before pursuing a post graduate course in PR.

I was working towards pursuing a master's in International Relations when a chance conversation with Ravi Dubey changed the course of things. Dubey was a Tata Administrative Services (TAS) officer, an immensely charismatic person with a flair for communications, who later went on to head corporate affairs at the Indian Hotels Company Limited. At that time he was the CEO of the PR firm, Good Relations India Ltd, and hearing him speak about the varied and significant mandates that the consultancy worked on, got me interested to learn more about PR and eventually study towards taking it up as a career option. After earning a postgraduate diploma in PR from Bhartiya Vidya Bhavan, I started my career at Good Relations.

One of the most defining phases of my career came when I moved to Dubai to join the Al Tayer Group, where I worked for nine years. I managed communications support for seven countries in the Middle-East region, necessitating a sound understanding of policy, political environment and cultural nuances, apart from knowledge of the media landscape.

Returning to India, I went on to lead two of the country's most respected PR consultancies— Dentsu Perfect Relations (now Dentsu Creative PR) and Madison PR. At Perfect Relations, I helped steer a legacy firm into a new chapter of its history. The process of transition from an independent consultancy to becoming a Dentsu India brand was both exciting and challenging for me as the CEO.

What set Madison PR apart was not just its capability but its fine culture, where learning was encouraged and fear of failure did not keep us from pursuing a worthy idea. As part of the Madison World ecosystem, the firm enjoyed an edge in being able to offer integrated services from within the group companies.

There were several campaigns I worked on, of which two stand out for me. One involved crisis communications support over an extended period of time for a reputed atta brand. A malicious video claimed that the atta from that brand contained plastic; that if the dough made from it was washed several times in water, it resulted in an elastic-like substance (claimed to be plastic), which caused panic and confusion among lakhs of viewers. A protein, gluten, naturally found in wheat flour was being misrepresented as plastic in the branded atta. Multiple videos making similar claims mushroomed across the country. It took a regionally differentiated strategy to address each of the local and hyperlocal markets that saw the issue erupt. Swift and decisive actions from all stakeholders involved led to ensuring that the desired communications objectives were accomplished; fake news was addressed, and the issue contained effectively. This reputation management campaign went on to win top honours at several PR awards.

I joined HDFC Bank in March 2022, once again coming back to an in-house role. Corporate India's largest merger in recent history was announced within a fortnight of my joining the bank, adding a whole new dimension to the communications role and responsibilities. I'd like to believe that several milestones have been crossed well over the years, working alongside some very fine professionals at the bank.

In summary, I will add that the setbacks or challenges I faced over the last three decades have provided me the opportunity to reflect and learn. I learnt that having all the ingredients does not guarantee the perfect dish, and the same goes for success. The importance of hard work, reading widely and attention to detail cannot be underestimated.

To young professionals entering this field, I offer this: do not wait for the perfect plan. Let curiosity lead you. Read widely. Listen carefully. Work hard. The career you build may not look like anyone else's, and that's a good thing. The most enduring journeys often begin without a map.

Mine certainly did. And I would not change a thing.

# 15

# Shravani Dang

## FORMER GLOBAL VICE PRESIDENT - GROUP COMMUNICATIONS, AVANTHA GROUP

---

*'The joy comes from knowing I have helped create opportunities and provided support when it was needed, giving others the confidence to take risks and pursue their own goals.'*

I WAS BORN IN KOLKATA AND SPENT MUCH OF MY CHILDHOOD in what was then the Bengal Principality, as my father was an IAS officer in the Bihar cadre. This meant I lived in small towns, in large colonial bungalows, with huge gardens and lots of animals.

I spent a lot of time reading. My father would often read aloud to us at the dinner table, encouraging us to find topics to discuss and research, even though there was no internet or phone to help us. It taught us to think critically, though we sometimes tried to wing it and got caught when we did not know enough!

We moved to Delhi, where I attended the Convent of Jesus and Mary, but it was a rather sheltered life. Growing up, both my parents instilled values that went beyond just academic achievements. My father's family was full of writers, poets and freedom fighters, while my mother's family were doctors. I come from a unique mix of backgrounds that shaped my perspective on the world.

When we moved to Delhi, my mother faced challenges in her career because of her Bengali accent. Once, when she mispronounced a name at her new job, the reaction from others led her to quit. From that experience, my parents taught us not to judge others by superficial traits but to focus on substance—what truly matters is the content, not how it's delivered. And that respect is key for relationships, both personal and official. These lessons have stayed with me throughout my life, and I carry it with me to this day.

I went to Miranda House for college and studied sociology, believing that understanding Indian culture was vital if I wanted to become a journalist. I later went to the Indian Institute of Mass Communications and graduated in 1981.

I was recruited to my first job straight from college. I joined HCL, which at the time was still very much a start-up. We had only one telephone, and all of us fought for a chance to use it. There were not enough chairs. I spent ten years there, and during that time, I got a lot of exposure to various aspects of communications, including marketing and CSR. At the time, there were no PR firms or event management agencies, so I had to handle everything.

I started as a trainee, and within six months, I was confirmed as an executive. HCL was ahead of its time in understanding the importance of communications. They knew the value of storytelling and creating the right narrative and were very forward-thinking when it came to marketing. The leadership was fantastic, and I learnt a lot, especially from the open atmosphere where you could walk into anyone's room with an idea or a problem. Sure, sometimes the ideas were rejected, but it was a great learning environment.

One of my most memorable experiences was during a campaign we were running for HCL's hardware sales. Advertising was part of what we did, and we were preparing for a big campaign to launch in March, as it was the time when most machines were sold. My boss and I worked together to come up with the campaign artwork. At a meeting with senior leaders to present the idea, one of the big bosses seemed distracted, but I was so confident in my idea that I stuck to my guns. At twenty-one or twenty-two, I thought I could change the world. When they questioned my approach, I defended it by explaining my reasoning in detail. They listened, acknowledged the good points, but pointed out something I had not considered. They told me I had twenty-four hours to incorporate their feedback, and I did. It was before automation, so everything had to be done manually. I remember working through it all, and the sense of accomplishment when it was successfully completed was incredible.

After my time at HCL, I decided to take a break and founded a creative writing workshop. After some time, I returned to the corporate world but not directly. I first joined an international NGO called CARE, which focuses on philanthropy and charity. I had a fulfilling role there before being headhunted by a company called Computer Sciences Corporation (CSC), a major player in software that worked alongside IBM. I thrived in that leadership team and later moved to Fidelity to oversee their communications operations in India.

At Fidelity, I was part of the India leadership team and reported to my boss in the UK, even though Fidelity's headquarters was in Boston. At the time, global operations were managed from the UK, so I frequently communicated with both Boston and the UK teams.

After Fidelity, I moved to the Thapar Group, where I took on the role of chief communications officer (CCO) with the designation of vice president global. One of the key reasons I joined was that I had worked in technology, development and in financial sectors but never in a conglomerate or manufacturing.

I spent over ten years at the now renamed Avantha Group and also served as an advisor to Thapar University.

In my last job, I was fortunate to have an incredible mentor. My chairman was very passionate about balanced leadership and encouraged women to achieve their ambitions and reach their potential. At that time, there were no women in the senior-most leadership team. I worked hard and had a voice and a presence in key discussions. I earned a seat at the table in a male-dominated hundred-year-old organisation. I also had a fantastic leadership coach, Mala Bali, who was truly exceptional. She played a huge role in shaping my approach to leadership.

As I reflect on my career, I have realised that life's lessons often provide the most profound education, even more than formal training. For example, when it comes to hiring, I would always urge caution against making snap judgements based solely on resumes from well-known colleges or brands. Often, true talent is hidden in unexpected places. By keeping an open mind, I was fortunate to find some truly remarkable people.

There are many more success stories, and for me, this is the greatest achievement. Mentoring, guiding and enabling others to succeed is truly invaluable. The joy comes from knowing I have helped create opportunities and provided support when it was needed, giving others the confidence to take risks and pursue their own goals. If they faltered along the way, I was there to catch them, and that's something I will always be proud of.

# 16

# Anuj Dayal

PRINCIPAL EXECUTIVE DIRECTOR - CORPORATE COMMUNICATIONS, DELHI METRO RAIL CORPORATION LTD.

---

*'I delegate extensively, and I believe in empowering my team. I invest a lot in training, and I trust my people fully.'*

I WAS BORN IN DELHI IN A MILITARY HOSPITAL, AS MY FATHER was in the army. I studied in Delhi until Class 7. After that, we moved to Bangalore, where I completed ICSE Class 10 from St Joseph's School. We later returned to Delhi, and I graduated from DPS Mathura Road before attending Hindu College.

After my graduation, I appeared for the civil services examination and was selected. I joined the Indian Railways, where I discovered the public relations department. I found PR much more exciting than the usual government work and managed to get involved in it. Prior to this, I had pursued several diplomas—about six or seven in total—covering PR, advertising, personnel management, marketing and tourism. At the time (1984–90), formal degrees in PR or mass communication were not widely available, and courses were mostly offered through institutions like the Indian Institute of Mass Communication and Bhartiya Vidya Bhavan.

I briefly worked as a reporter for a Mumbai-based food magazine, where I had the opportunity to write a few articles that got published. Looking back, if I had not joined the civil services, I believe I would have pursued a career in journalism.

I spent nearly a decade in the PR wing of Indian Railways. Towards the end of my time there, the Delhi Metro Project was starting, and they were looking for someone to manage PR for it. The project was a massive urban development effort within Delhi, and given the significant media presence in the capital, it required a skilled communications professional to handle PR.

I was selected for the position. Initially, I was reluctant to join and even declined the offer. However, after a meeting with E. Sreedharan, who led the Konkan Railway and the Delhi Metro, I reconsidered and eventually accepted the role. I have no regrets since then. It's been twenty-seven years, and I have been heading the corporate communications for Delhi Metro, which started as a one-man team. Today, our team has grown to about twenty-five people and continues to expand, especially with the rise of social and alternate media.

I joined in 1998, just after the company really began to take off as Dr Sreedharan became the MD in November 1997. For the first ten years, I operated with a very small team of only four people. We managed and built the entire Delhi Metro brand internally, without spending money on advertising. Over the last twenty-seven years, we have relied solely on in-house PR, with no dependence on external PR firms.

When I began at Delhi Metro, media relations was mostly centred around print media, with television being limited to Doordarshan. However, with the arrival of private players like NDTV, the media landscape began to shift. In those early days, print had well-established procedures for redressal, with tools like letters to the editor, but TV required a different approach. TV was faster-paced and news would appear and disappear quickly, making it harder to address issues once they were aired. As a communicator, I had to be extremely cautious about what I said, knowing that any portion of an interview could be edited and used out of context later.

There were some dramatic moments, especially during the early years. For instance, once my office was surrounded by electronic media because they were not invited to a particular press conference. Some even demanded that I be removed from my position. Fortunately, I had strong backing from Delhi's then chief minister, the late Sheila Dikshit, and Sreedharan, who gave me full support at that time.

However, a major turning point came when a tragic accident in South Delhi claimed the lives of nine workers. The pressure mounted significantly, and I was handling everything alone at that time. For two days straight, I was on the phone for almost twenty-four hours each day, fielding endless calls, particularly from TV journalists where the beat system is not as structured as in print. This intense workload began affecting my health, and I realised I could no longer manage everything on my own.

That's when I decided to expand the team. I developed a system where I divided media responsibilities among my officers—one person handles English papers, another manages Hindi, someone takes care of TV, radio and social media. All communication is cleared by me, ensuring consistency and accuracy in everything we release. No information goes out without my approval, and I maintain direct contact with the CEO to ensure smooth communication.

As the Delhi Metro continued to grow—now the largest metro network in India with over 400 kilometres of track—our communication needs expanded. We were instrumental in building a museum at Patel Chowk.

The critical part of my job is ensuring that our communication is swift and accurate, especially during service disruptions, where even a slight delay needs immediate attention. Beyond that, I continue to handle construction communications as we are still building, even after twenty-five years.

One of the things I'm most proud of is how we have maintained a positive reputation of the project. I take complex technical information, whether it is civil engineering or signalling, and convert it into reader-friendly stories. This has helped us secure front-page coverage in leading papers. By doing so, we have gained the support of the public, and naturally, political and bureaucratic backing followed, allowing the project to progress smoothly.

A major challenge we faced was in 2002 when the metro was first introduced in socio-economically disadvantaged areas of Delhi. These were neighbourhoods where people did not read newspapers, so traditional PR and media would not be enough to encourage them to use the system. The metro was a very modern concept at the time. There were no escalators in Delhi back then, except at the international airport and at one hotel. The system had automatic ticketing, fare collection gates and automatic train doors, all of which seemed intimidating to people who had never encountered such technology.

Indeed, communication in these early days was about much more than just traditional PR—it was about finding ways to reach people in ways that resonated with them and helped them adapt to something entirely new.

You need someone dedicated full-time, either in-house or from a consultancy, who really understands the organisation and can maximise opportunities. There's so much more that a dedicated person can uncover and share. Years ago, I was completely reliant on external media—newspapers, radio or TV—to get our news out. If my management wanted something published, I had to go through these outlets. My success depended entirely on how much coverage I could secure through them.

Today, things are different. With social media under our control, we can reach out directly. Plus, online editions of newspapers provide much more space, making it easier to get news out. It's much simpler now to create an impact compared to earlier days. With our own social media channels, we can consistently push out content and make sure the message is visible. When you combine all of this, management sees the constant flow of posts and activity, and it creates a strong impression.

I delegate extensively, and I believe in empowering my team. I invest a lot in training, and I trust my people fully. In fact, 99 per cent of the time, my judgement and assessment of people have been spot-on. Of course, there are always a few individuals who cannot be helped, and in those cases, it's best to part ways and move on. But for the rest, I focus on developing them. I keep a close watch but do not micro-manage. My team knows I'm paying attention, and if mistakes happen, I usually correct them—provided the intentions are good.

# 17

# Deepa Dey

## Former Head - Corporate Communications, Airtel

---

*'My career journey has been shaped largely by partnership and passion.'*

I was born into a conservative business family in Kolkata. The business was started by my uncle and my father. Our origin can be traced back to Dhaka, Bangladesh, from where my parents had migrated to India when they were very young. India became home and they settled down and over a period of time the family business, The Radiant Process, was set up. It became one of the leading printing presses in India.

As a master's student, I was regularly writing for the Metro section of *The Economic Times*, working with Reshmi Dasgupta and Nandini Sengupta. From a mehendi festival to a deep dive into the morgue, I had done whatever came my way. Seeing one's byline in the papers was a high. During this time, I also saw an ad in the newspaper about *Amrit Bazaar*

*Patrika*, India's first English publication owned by Indians, which was about to relaunch as a colour newspaper. A friend and I applied, and we were selected to be trained in desktop publishing, which was a new and exciting skill at the time. We were, however, trained in typewriting and my speed was sixty-five words! This was in the early days of computer-based publishing, and I was fascinated by the idea of producing an entire newspaper from a computer. Though I worked there for a short time, I acquired a new skill.

Then one day a headhunter reached out about a position at the Park Hotels in Kolkata in public relations. I had no idea what PR was, so I asked, 'How much will they pay?' The headhunter assured me that I could name my price and they would match it. So, I went for the interview and got the job.

At that point, I had two offers in hand—*The Statesman*, a prestigious publication with a rich legacy, and the Park Hotels, which offered slightly more money. My father was thrilled about *The Statesman*, but I chose the Park Hotels, partly because of the salary and partly out of curiosity to explore PR.

I ended up staying with the Park Hotels for four years, heading their PR function with no prior experience in the field. My first day in PR was as the head of the Communications Department and I did not know how hotels operated beyond being a guest, but I was thrown into the deep end. I had a great set of colleagues.

Priya Paul and Priti Paul took a punt on me, gave me new projects to work on, allowing me to grow in my own way. After four grateful years, I felt the need to expand my horizons and moved to Mumbai, where I joined Clea Public Relations. I joined Clea as senior consultant. My first day was an offsite at the Arey Milk Colony where Sunil Gautam, one of the founders, introduced me to Nikhil Dey at the breakfast table. Yes, we met on the first day, but we largely kept out of each other's way till I started handling Philips India Limited, which was a marquee client for the company.

My time at Clea was short—less than two years—but it was important for my learning. Working at a consultancy opened my eyes to the possibilities of PR in a way that corporate roles hadn't thus far. Working with a corporate, I had been blinkered into unidirectional learning, which literally exploded when I was in a consultancy, dealing with multiple clients and issues.

After getting married and moving to Delhi, I reconnected with Priya Paul, my former boss. I was ready to take on something new. She invited me to join her, to build the corporate communications function for the entire Apeejay Surrendra Group. The group had a wide range of business interests—from hospitality, real estate, retail to financial services, shipping and tea. I built the function from the ground up, hiring and expanding the team, and stayed for seven years, working across Mumbai and Delhi. We launched new hotels and bookstores across India. I worked on e-commerce when it was not a thing. I worked on a business centre with 'hot desking' much before the concept hit the market. And that was huge!

A significant personal shift occurred during this time—I became a mother. Every stage in life is accompanied with a change and a challenge, but nothing was as tectonic as that of being a mother. I moved out of Delhi with a tiny Neil (he was less than a month old) to be with my in-laws, while Nikhil was setting up home for us in Mumbai, working with Fiat.

I spent about two-and-a-half years in Mumbai during this period, managing multiple high-profile events before moving back to Delhi when Nikhil joined Genesis PR. I continued with Apeejay Surrendra Group—moving back to the head office in Pragati Bhavan.

After seven long years working closely with Priya, Priti and Karan Paul, I decided to step away from my job, needing some time to be with my son. Motherhood makes strange demands and parenting is not easy. The Pauls were incredibly understanding, and I handed over to a very efficient team and moved on.

After a short break of four months, I joined SpiceJet, a three-year-old company as old as my son! And it was closer home. This was my first stint with a listed entity and I understood that nuances of the role. Interestingly, the role offered an exciting shift—the company wanted me to join not as the head of communications alone, but as the head of communications and organisation culture. I stayed for a little over two years, during which time we went through two rounds of fund infusion and a change in leadership.

While I was at SpiceJet, I received a call from Airtel. The company wanted to talk to me about the role of head of communications. My time at Airtel, spanning three-and-a-half years, was a period of spectacular learning. Very few stints give so much at such pace and precision as this one did. The scale and complexity of the work was at a different level. There was never a pause. Promoting campaigns like 'Har Ek Friend Zaroori Hota Hain' to dealing with undersea cable cut to losing connectivity in the city of Mumbai during the year end—there were many learnings with eight consultancies and twenty-two team members across three countries. In addition to all these, there were regulatory challenges.

In 2013, GSK Consumer Healthcare was looking for a head of communications for the Indian subcontinent. The headhunter reached out to me, and I was open to evaluating. I had never worked for an MNC before, and many of my Airtel colleagues, most ex-Unilever, had always spoken very highly of GSK. At Airtel, while I was a part of the company leadership, I was not on the management board. With GSK, I was a part of the country management board, responsible for the area P&L and head of the function.

I was really happy at GSK working with amazing people. On 27 March 2018, GSK Consumer Healthcare's nutrition business went under strategic review, which ultimately led to its sale to Unilever. I concluded my stint at Unilever in July 2024, after four fabulous years with one of the leading organisations in the world.

When I look back at my thirty and beyond years of being in active work phase, I feel an immense sense of gratitude for everything the universe has allowed me to achieve. I consider myself incredibly fortunate. I have maintained wonderful relationships with every organisation I have worked with, and though I may not be in constant contact with everyone, I know that if I ever need help, they will be there for me. Some of these relationships have even turned into close friendships—almost like family.

# 18

# Meenu Handa

VICE PRESIDENT - COMMUNICATIONS, GOOGLE

---

*'Each chapter—whether in communications, technology, retail, or consumer branding—has added depth and diversity to my professional journey.'*

I WAS BORN AND RAISED IN DELHI AND AM DEEPLY ROOTED there. My father worked with the State Bank of India, while my mother, a dedicated professional, served as a lady health visitor with the Municipal Corporation of Delhi. Both my parents faced significant struggles. They came to Delhi during Partition—not as refugees, but as Indians navigating a difficult time. Their resilience and hard work built a stable and comfortable life for us even though they started out with very little. When they got married, they returned from their honeymoon with only 50 paise in their bank account, yet they gave us a life rich in values and opportunities. Watching them work tirelessly instilled in me a deep appreciation for hard work and perseverance. Moreover, my mother's unwavering commitment to her career and her indomitable spirit while raising three children was a constant source of inspiration for me.

Basketball too played a pivotal role in shaping who I am. I started playing basketball at the young age of eleven and met some of my closest friends on the court. Basketball taught me teamwork and the ability to bounce back after setbacks. You do not win every game, but the real lesson is in showing up, trying again and building self-confidence. And it was my love of the sport and the competitive level at which I was playing that led me to decide to stay back in Delhi to pursue my passion for the sport, even as my family moved to the UK for a few years. Eventually, I achieved my dream of playing for India.

My career in communications was serendipitous. After college at St Stephen's, I was at a crossroads, exploring options in business development and advertising while considering pursuing the civil services. I was not entirely certain about my path and did not want to pursue a master's degree, so I kept looking for opportunities.

A chance meeting with an old friend led me to Rama Lakshmi, who was taking a course in PR and journalism at the Bhartiya Vidya Bhavan, Delhi. It seemed like the perfect fit for me, so I joined the evening classes while preparing for the civil services. Though I was not serious about the exams and did not crack them, this phase helped me discover my interest in communications. That decision set off on my career trajectory. Ever since, it has been a mix of passion, hard work and fortunate opportunities.

After completing my course, I found myself wondering, what next? That's when I came across a feature in *India Today* about the communications profession, which was emerging at the time, and IPAN's role in it. Inspired, I decided to apply there. However, Rajiv Desai, who headed IPAN, told me there was no space in the office at the time. They were a small operation and planned to expand after moving to a bigger office.

Undeterred, I pursued the opportunity relentlessly. For six months, I called every week to check if there was any update. Eventually, I think Rajiv grew tired of my persistence and finally offered me a position—albeit with a catch. There was no desk available, so I was given space at the reception. I gladly accepted. Another colleague, Vanita Mishra, and I started on the same day, both sitting at the reception due to the lack of physical space. Interestingly, the moment I walked into IPAN, I knew this was what I wanted to do long-term.

The early 1990s were an exciting time for the profession. Liberalisation had opened India to global businesses, and IPAN, affiliated with Hill & Knowlton and part of JWT, was at the forefront of this transformation. The exposure was incredible—working with brands like Boeing, Star TV, Swatch group, Unilever, HCL and several other leading companies across industries gave me invaluable experience. IPAN itself was just a couple of years old when I joined, and the profession had just started to bloom, and so all three of us, IPAN, the profession and I grew together. Over fifteen years, I progressed from a management trainee to vice president, forming lifelong relationships and learning from an exceptional set of colleagues and clients.

While there are many projects that stand out as truly transformative and fulfilling experiences in these fifteen years, there are two I feel most proud about and can share. One was leading campaigns for duty and tax reductions, notably for cosmetics and toiletries, as well as for tea. These were separate campaigns, but both aimed at reducing excise duties. The cosmetics campaign was particularly memorable, as it involved a unique combination of communications, stakeholder engagement and collaboration with allies like consumer and women's groups. Partnering with Anil Chopra, who headed Lakmé at the time, we crafted a narrative that resonated deeply. Hearing the campaign's core messages echoed in the then Finance Minister Manmohan Singh's budget speech as he announced the duty reduction was a professional high like no other.

The second one was the six years we spent building the Star TV brand. In the early years as a consultancy, we were responsible for starting the cable industry business. Besides communications, we were the de facto office for producers and advertisers. Star TV's first office was hosted within the IPAN office. There can be no bigger endorsement for a firm. This was the brand that honed my marketing skills, thanks to Ann Tsang, who was the publicity/PR manager for Star TV.

And then a moment came when I realised I had never experienced another workplace culture. IPAN's culture was deeply embedded within me, and I felt it was time to broaden my horizons. Around the same time, Microsoft was looking for someone to lead its communications function in India, and Prema Sagar (founder of Genesis), referred me. I met with Ravi Venkatesan (then head of Microsoft India), and everything fell in place. I joined Microsoft in 2005, marking a new chapter in my career.

At Microsoft, I transitioned from the breadth of consultancy work to the depth of corporate communications. It was a fascinating learning curve. I developed expertise in internal communications, a domain I hadn't explored before. Working with cross-functional teams—including legal, policy and marketing—I created a stakeholder engagement programme and led initiatives like accessibility communications. Microsoft approached communications with scientific precision, and I gained immense knowledge about structured global practices during my seven-and-a-half years there.

Around the time I began to feel that I had gained all I could at Microsoft, I was approached by Amazon. A former colleague from Microsoft recommended me, and I joined as the communications leader as Amazon was getting ready to launch in India. My three years there were transformative. Amazon's approach to communications was the polar opposite of Microsoft's—it was an art form. The role was extremely empowering and allowed me to innovate and adapt in ways I hadn't experienced before. In the early years. I was able to take on some elements of marketing communications and also create a CSR stream for the company, broadening my scope beyond anything I had done previously.

Then came an opportunity with Google. Initially, I said no, as I was really enjoying my stint at Amazon, a great company with an incredible brand. However, the recruiter was persistent and persuasive. He pointed out that very few people had the chance to carry the trifecta of Microsoft, Amazon and Google on their resumes. It was a compelling argument, and I eventually gave in. Vanity aside, I saw the potential to make a meaningful impact at Google. So, nine-and-a-half years ago, I joined Google to lead their communications team in India.

At Google, I joined a small team but quickly received support to grow it. After a couple of years, I moved to Singapore to oversee India and Southeast Asia. With a strong successor in place for India, I worked on initiatives like the launch of Google Pay globally and the Next Billion Users programme. This role expanded into markets across Africa, Latin America and Asia-Pacific. Since the global leadership for these programmes was based in Singapore, it made sense to manage them from there.

As Google shifted priorities, I transitioned to an APAC-wide role, first as an interim leader and eventually taking it on full-time. And since then, my team began our transition to becoming a communications team that was in sync with changing consumer habits and the tech world well ahead of many in the industry. We have created new platforms, developed new formats, reached new audiences and leveraged every tool to amplify our impact, both internally and externally. And all of this while navigating everyday complexities.

Overall, I look back with profound fulfilment and gratitude, and all of this is directly attributable to the exceptional teams I have worked with and the steadfast trust of my clients, managers and stakeholders.

# 19

# Mahesh Jayaram

## Director & Head - Corporate Communications, Dell Technologies India

*'Storytelling has always been a core passion of mine, and I firmly believe that a compelling, differentiated narrative is at the heart of effective communication.'*

I WAS BORN IN MYSORE, OFTEN CALLED THE 'CITY OF Palaces', where I spent my early years before moving to Bangalore. Mysore holds a special place in my heart, filled with fond memories. I completed my schooling in Bangalore and later pursued a degree in electrical engineering from the National Institute of Engineering, Mysore.

I come from a close-knit family. I have a younger brother and sister. My parents played a significant role in shaping my values. My father was a civil engineer and architect, while my mother was a homemaker. We had a happy and fulfilling childhood. I am married to Babita, a talented restaurateur specialising in creating and setting up concept restaurants. We have a daughter, Maanya. A special member of our family is our Shih Tzu, Leo.

Professionally, I have over three decades of experience spanning public relations, marketing, sales and advertising. I have had the privilege of working with marquee companies such as Dell Technologies, IBM, British Telecom and GE Medical Systems. My transition into PR and communications was driven by a deep passion for storytelling and brand building. My early roles at GE Medical Systems and British Telecom helped shape my expertise in media relations, corporate messaging and stakeholder management.

Today, I play a key role in shaping corporate messaging, branding, thought leadership, brand reputation, business and trade media relations, channel partner communications and executive visibility. At Dell Technologies, I oversee both internal and external communications. Beyond work, I have a few passions that I actively pursue. I'm an avid collector of fountain pens and have been practising calligraphy for over two decades. I also have a deep appreciation for mechanical watches.

Reflecting on my career, I find one defining moment that shaped my perspective occurred during my early days at GE Medical Systems. At the time, GE was at its peak, led by Jack Welch. We were participating in the Asian Oceanian Congress of Radiology (AOCR) at Pragati Maidan, one of the largest radiology trade shows, held once every four years. I was tasked with managing our media presence, press tours and overall event execution.

A major logistical challenge arose when our medical equipment—CT scanners, MRI machines and ultrasound scanners—shipped from different parts of the world, got stuck at customs due to an issue with compliance documentation.

The president of India was scheduled to inaugurate the event, and we were in a race against time.

On the advice of our freight forwarder, we approached the US Embassy in New Delhi. Within minutes of explaining the situation, the commercial attaché made a few calls and assured us that the equipment would be released. The US Embassy stood as a guarantor for GE, stating, 'GE is a jewel in the US crown, and we will not let you down.'

This experience deeply impacted me, demonstrating the immense power of brand reputation. It reinforced my belief in the influence a well-established brand carries, something I have carried with me throughout my career.

I'd like to share some of my key learnings and experiences—moments that left a lasting impression and shaped my understanding of high-level communications and influencer engagement. One such experience was during my time at British Telecom when we participated in 'Telecom 95', a major industry event. At the time, India's telecom sector was still at a nascent stage, and we were focused on the VSAT business. The event, held in Geneva, opened my eyes to the scale and sophistication of global influencer engagement.

As part of our strategy, we hosted 200 top customers and key media representatives at the Royal du Golfe Palace Hotel, a luxurious resort near Evian, the source of the famed mineral water. From there, guests were flown by helicopter to Geneva, where a luxury yacht anchored on Lake Geneva served as the venue for an exclusive engagement.

The highlight of the evening was a dining experience like no other—an authentic dining car from the historic Orient Express was set up on the banks of Lake Geneva, creating an unforgettable atmosphere. Witnessing the precision with which these engagements were executed, the meticulous attention to detail and the powerful impact they had on media and customer relationships was truly inspiring.

One campaign that stands out in my journey was the launch of the IBM ThinkPad TransNote—a revolutionary device ahead of its time. It allowed users to write on a tablet, automatically transcribing notes into a digital document, which could then be emailed or shared.

To bring this innovation to life, we designed an experiential launch event that blended art, fashion and technology. We invited celebrated personalities—cartoonist Mario Miranda, author Shobhaa De, actress Lillete Dubey and fashion designer Hemant Trivedi, who had just designed gowns for the Miss World pageant.

The event featured a live demonstration where Mario Miranda sketched Hemant Trivedi's gown designs directly onto the TransNote. As his sketches appeared on a large screen in real time, models wearing the same designs walked into the audience, seamlessly merging art and technology. Shobhaa De and Lillete Dubey further elevated the experience by performing a skit using the TransNote, showcasing its versatility.

This launch was held at iconic venues like the India Habitat Centre in Delhi and the Taj Mahal Palace Hotel in Mumbai, receiving widespread acclaim. It was a powerful example of storytelling done right, transforming a tech product into an experience that resonated deeply with both media and influencers.

I'd like to share another example, this time from Delhi. One particular initiative that stands out is a sustainability campaign we designed called #BlackistheNewGreen. Across India, offices rely heavily on diesel generators due to frequent power cuts. These generators release harmful black smoke, a major environmental and health hazard. To address this, we partnered with Chakr Innovation, a Delhi-based start-up founded by three IIT Delhi graduates. Their groundbreaking technology captured the diesel generator fumes and converted them into non-toxic ink.

We used this ink to print all the packaging boxes from our Dell factory in Sriperumbudur, Chennai. So far, over 150,000 boxes have been printed using this eco-friendly PO Ink—a powerful example of sustainability in action. To bring this story to life, we hosted an event at the New Metro Amphitheatre in Bangalore. We collaborated with upcoming fashion designer Tehra Peran, who used the ink to create stunning prints on gowns worn by her models. Additionally, Ponnappa, the renowned cartoonist, performed live sketching using the same ink, illustrating themes of environmental conservation. The event was more than just a presentation; it was an immersive experience. We engaged the media with a fireside chat, open discussions and interactive storytelling—moving beyond conventional press releases to create a lasting impact.

Throughout my career, I have often leveraged theatre, creativity and innovation to craft compelling narratives. I believe that effective storytelling goes beyond words; it needs to be experienced.

Over the years, I have followed a few core principles that have shaped my approach to communication: a) Be the voice, not the echo. Authentic communication is far more impactful than simply following trends. b) Anticipate, do not just react. PR is not just about crisis management; it's about proactively shaping and protecting a reputation. The ability to foresee challenges is an essential skill. c) Constantly evolve. The best communicators embrace change, technology and innovative storytelling. Staying ahead means continuously sharpening your skills.

If I were to share three key lessons for aspiring PR professionals, they would be: a) Master the art of storytelling. At its core, PR is about crafting compelling stories with a purpose. b) Invest in relationships. Whether it's with the media, influencers or stakeholders, strong relationships take time to build and require genuine effort. c) Stay curious and keep learning. The PR landscape is always evolving. The most successful professionals are lifelong learners who adapt and grow with the profession.

# 20

# Ritu Jhingon

FORMER GROUP DIRECTOR - COMMUNICATION,
VEDANTA

―⁂―

*'A life full of discipline, dreams and determination.'*

I WAS BORN IN NEW DELHI ON A COLD JANUARY NIGHT IN 1967—a night that became a story my family would carry for a lifetime. On 24 January, amidst Delhi's notorious winter fog, my mother, accompanied by my uncle, was en route to the military hospital when the taxi they were in overturned. At the time, Delhi had just a handful of prominent hotels, and one of them, the Ashoka Hotel, stood near the accident site. A group of waiters returning home on a Lambretta and bicycles noticed flickering lights in the distance and rushed to help. One of them pulled my mother out of the wreckage and ensured she reached the hospital. My uncle, though injured, followed shortly after, helped by the others. That night, I was born—just after midnight on 25 January.

In the chaos of the incident, no one told my mother about my arrival at first. In those days, especially in times of trauma, the birth of a girl was not always celebrated. But my mother, already a mother to a son, gently asked, 'Can you tell me?' And the nurse replied, 'You have a girl. And she's fine.'

Raised in a home where discipline was not just taught but lived, my upbringing was shaped by my father's career in the Indian Air Force and my mother's journey as an educator—rising from teacher to principal and eventually working with the Delhi administration. If there is one mantra that defines my journey, it is discipline. It's not a habit acquired later in life. It's a foundation laid early in life.

I was an active sportsperson—by thirteen, a state-level swimmer; by sixteen, competing nationally; and by seventeen, the head girl of my school. My mother was ahead of her time. When I once told her that I should learn cooking like other girls, she replied, 'You can pay someone 500 bucks to cook. Use your time to learn something more valuable.' She encouraged me to take a computer course at NIIT instead. That one decision shaped the way I approached my future—always with a focus on value, not convention.

In school, while most students gravitated towards science or arts, I chose commerce, determined to step into the business world. My time at SRCC—India's top commerce college—further sharpened my ambition. Simultaneously, I began hosting youth shows for All India Radio's Yuvavani, which honed my communication and voice modulation skills.

At twenty-three, I married my best friend. We had known each other for years, and together, we built a life that spanned cities and continents. Our son, born in 1994, is now a doctor—a quiet reminder that every generation can soar higher with the right foundation.

My husband's career with Indian Oil Corporation took us to Delhi, Chandigarh, Sri Lanka, Mumbai and back again. In every new city, I adapted and grew. In Chandigarh, I worked in advertising with Response Advertising, handling major clients like Coca-Cola. In Sri Lanka, I joined Ogilvy & Mather under Sandhya Salgado. Initially hesitant to hire an Indian, she offered me an unpaid trial.

One of the most defining projects I led was the replication of Hindustan Unilever's Shakti campaign in Sri Lanka—a women's empowerment initiative that not only boosted sales but transformed lives. It was my first deep dive into social impact communication, and it shaped my understanding of how storytelling and strategy can drive change.

Back in India, I joined *Hindustan Times*, leading marketing and brand strategy. I was part of the team that revamped *Hindustan Times* and *Mint*, and helped shape the iconic Hindustan Times Leadership Summit—interacting with global leaders, prime ministers and industry giants.

Later, Cairn India came calling. I knew little about the oil and gas industry then—except that my husband worked in one—but Cairn valued my Sri Lanka experience. I joined and soon transitioned to Vedanta, where I led communications across seventeen businesses.

In 2013, a call went out to all vertical leaders to move to Barmer in Rajasthan. Everyone said, 'You'll never survive in a village.' I volunteered. I spent three years in Barmer, commuting back to Delhi on weekends, while my husband was in Nigeria and my son in Bangalore. Those years changed me.

Today, at fifty-eight, my focus is on mentorship. I speak at forums, guide the next generation and share not just my victories—but my missteps too. I tell young professionals that adaptability is your greatest strength. Keep learning. Keep evolving.

And to women in corporate India, I want to say, resilience matters more than resistance. For every 10,000 men in leadership, only 1,500 women hold positions—and most are still in support roles. To thrive, we have had to be twice as good, work twice as hard and smile through it all. The journey has been uphill, but every step forward has been worth it.

# 21

# Narahari K.S.

### Former Director - Corporate Communications, Texas Instruments

*'I believe in the power of teamwork and leading from the front.'*

I WAS BORN IN KOLAR GOLD FIELDS, HUNDRED KILOMETRES from Bangalore. Life in the Bharat Gold Mines colony, spread across 3,200 acres, was quite sedate. My father would go down over 10,000 feet into the bowels of the earth every day with his team to extract the yellow metal. It was a difficult profession fraught with danger, with injuries and even fatalities occurring from time to time. When he started his career in the mid-1940s, even helmets were not in use. Miners would wear straw hats and work at high temperatures. Rock bursts (tunnels caving in deep under the ground) and fires were quite common. This made me realise the value of life at a rather young age.

There were only two schools in the mining colony—St Joseph's Convent for girls and KGF School for boys, so

I joined the latter. Our life in the 1960s followed a regular routine. Company-owned vans would take us to school in the morning and drop us at the Officers Club at 3.30 in the afternoon. Till 6.30 p.m., when the vans would return to pick us up, we would play badminton, tennis, or swim in the pool. Once a month, we would stay back for a movie show, mostly Charlie Chaplin and Laurel & Hardy comedies, or Walt Disney films. More than the movies, we would look forward to the chips and lemonade that were served in the interval. We have carried forward the great camaraderie even to this day.

Another highlight of our school days was the birthday parties that parents would organise in their respective bungalows built by John Taylor & Company, the erstwhile British owners of the mines.

Then I graduated from the University of Mysore. Later, I acquired postgraduate diplomas in public relations and journalism from Bharatiya Vidya Bhavan. From a young age, I wrote articles for our school and club magazines. Later in life, I wrote 'middles' in Deccan Herald and articles in various mainstream publications. I also have my own blog on cricket, a game that I have followed very closely.

A senior at school was working in the HR department of International Instruments in Bangalore. This company manufactured and sold the famous 'YenkaY' brand of automobile dashboard instruments that had a high market share across the country. In 1979, he placed me with the marketing communication team with the primary responsibility of contributing articles to their monthly journal. I also assisted the team in coordinating with the advertising agency that designed and produced collateral for the sales team.

Writing was a constant companion till I retired from service in late 2014 after a long journey covering International

Instruments, Smith Kline & French (SK&F), HMT—International and Watch Marketing Group, Wipro, IBM India and ASEAN/South Asia, Dell India and Texas Instruments India. At SK&F, a pharmaceutical company that had the popular Iodex on its product portfolio, I revived their quarterly journal *Eskaynews* and introduced a monthly journal called *Fieldman*, targeted at their 500-strong medical representatives spread across India. At HMT Watch Marketing Group, I revived their quarterly journal *Time Keepers*. In Wipro, I introduced *WiproScan*, and at IBM, Dell and Texas Instruments, I was the scribe for internal communications as well as for contributing news reports and feature articles for their global publications. Right through my career, I was fortunate to get the opportunity to perform various functions covering marketing communications, corporate communications, industry analyst relations and corporate events.

In 1989, the Government of India approached HMT for an innovative way to commemorate the birth anniversary of Pandit Jawaharlal Nehru, our first prime minister. The company produced audio and video versions of songs extolling Pandit Nehru and national integration in eight Indian languages with HMT employees drawn from different units across India writing the lyrics and rendering the songs. I was nominated the coordinator for this unique project. It gave me the opportunity to work with professional videographers and editors, audio experts, music directors and particularly with renowned film star Waheeda Rehman, who anchored the two versions. Doordarshan and All India Radio included them in their Nehru centenary programmes.

Anything done for the first time remains deeply etched in memory and I had my own share of memorable firsts. I was the first corporate communications head for Wipro and IBM India and the first Indian citizen to head communications for Dell India, succeeding an expat from Singapore. I was also the first representative from Wipro-GE on the GE Medical Systems Asia Communication Board. At HMT Watch Marketing group, I carried out rural promotion of mechanical watches in North Bihar and the Malwa region of Madhya Pradesh, again a first for the company.

In 1997, during the India-Pakistan One Day International cricket match at the MA Chidambaram Stadium in Chennai, IBM was the first company to deploy cheerleaders from Stella Maris College, under my initiative and supervision, that probably set the trend for the future. A year earlier, we had attracted the IT industry's attention by erecting a large IBM neon sign on top of the rented building of Wipro Infotech on Bangalore's tony MG Road. Later, in 2004, I spearheaded an employee branding initiative at Dell's customer contact centres in Bangalore, Hyderabad, Mohali and Gurgaon that involved adorning the walls with giant posters of the company's young employees shot in picturesque locations, a first for Dell across the world.

Organising events are an integral part of a corporate communicator's portfolio, both internal and external. While it was mostly technology-related at IBM, at HMT Watch Marketing Group, it was all about consumers, with new product launches, including exclusive watches for the youth and young school children, watch gifting events for students excelling in academics and organising HMT booths at India International Trade Fair and other watch and clock exhibitions. Internal events included organising town halls for Michael Dell's (Dell Technologies chairman) and Rich Templeton's (Texas Instruments chairman) visits. Quite often, I would be given the task of arranging motivation talks by management 'gurus' and leading sports personalities. To commemorate Texas Instruments completing twenty-five years in India in 2010, I was given a year-long mandate to organise technical, cultural and family events with the help of a dedicated team drawn from various departments across the organisation.

In those days, media interactions were largely with print publications. The outcomes were completely organic—earned media. We did not have the paid, owned and shared versions that are prevalent today since technology and the internet had not made inroads yet. But the strong relationship that we forged with journalists was something to be cherished. We would always meet face-to-face. It was not uncommon to see corporate communications professionals regularly at media houses discussing story ideas and topics. The mutual trust was tremendous. Unfortunately, in these days of e-mails and WhatsApp messages, the personal touch is woefully missing.

The deep relationship with the media helped me when faced with crises. A timely tip-off from a mainstream journalist that the workers' union had called for a press conference that afternoon helped me quickly organise a press briefing. It was held in the basement of an under-construction hotel on Bangalore's St Marks Road when the company where I was working was going through a long-drawn strike resulting in a lock-out in the early 1990s. This helped us get the management's point of view in the reports that came out the next day.

From November 2014 to March 2025—after thirty-five years of corporate life, I ventured into the consultancy side of PR by joining The PRactice, a leading PR firm as a senior consultant. My long experience in technology companies fitted well with the firm's core strengths. At The PRactice, I got the opportunity to guide and mentor young professionals and help them in their career development. I also advised client-facing executives on media relations and discussed media strategies and campaigns with our clients' communication teams. I also conducted media training to the clients' leadership teams.

I earnestly believe that I have derived a lot from the communications profession, and therefore I have always had the desire to give back something in return. Towards this endeavour, I have been teaching communication-related subjects to students in different institutes.

I believe in the power of teamwork and leading from the front. I am convinced that I have stood by my colleagues in good and bad times. I have empowered them to make decisions so that they become effective leaders in the future. I have encouraged them to maintain a sharp focus and deliver on promises consistently, proving their reliability early in their career. And above everything else, I have urged them to protect their character, as integrity and trust are the greatest assets that one can possess.

To succeed in any profession, one must be passionate. Life is a long-drawn marathon and not a glamorous hundred-metre sprint. Pursuing traits like discipline, dedication and determination, along with honesty and hard work, is the only way to leave behind an indelible mark on future generations. More than anything else, one must learn to take success and failure with humility and magnanimity.

# 22

# Bharatendu Kabi

### EVP & Group Head - Media & Communications, JSW

―⁂―

*'Each step in my journey has shaped my perspective and strengthened my belief in the power of purposeful leadership and impactful communication.'*

I WAS BORN AND RAISED IN RAIRANGPUR. IT IS IN THE DISTRICT of Mayurbhanj in Odisha, which used to be a princely state ruled by the famed Bhanj Deo dynasty before its integration into the Union of India in 1948. It is just an hour's drive from the 'Steel City' of Jamshedpur and about five hours from Kolkata.

Born into a family of lawyers and academics, my two younger siblings—sister and brother in that order—and I had our early education in Rairangpur. Our first school was Purna Chandra Maharaja Upper Primary School, named after the erstwhile King of Mayurbhanj. For my graduation, I moved to Buxi Jagabandhu Bidyadhara (BJB) College in Odisha. After graduating from BJB College, I did my post-graduation in political science at Utkal University in Bhubaneswar. Like many students in the region at that time, I also briefly prepared for the civil services, primarily due to familial and societal expectations.

It was around this time that I came across a newspaper advertisement by the Press Trust of India. I applied and got the job at PTI. This changed the course of my life. On 1 April 1995, I joined as one of the trainee journalists at the Delhi bureau of PTI. That's how my life in Delhi started— with days of acute struggle and moments of intense joy in equal measure, silent battle with loneliness and the sheer joys of finding true friends, self-doubt and career highs, the eagerness to be accepted and the fear of rejection.

It was around early 1999 that I was exploring opportunities outside PTI, including very advanced discussions with a European newswire and a national newspaper. And then, an unexpected offer came my way. My editor—I will not name him here—approached me with a question that would ultimately change my career trajectory. He asked, 'Would you be interested in a corporate communications role at PepsiCo? I think you will make a good communicator.' He explained that they were not looking for a traditional PR professional but wanted someone with a media background.

While feeling very humbled with his words of appreciation and encouragement, I dismissed the idea outright. I was passionate about journalism and had no experience or interest in corporate communications. But my editor would not give up easily; encouraging me to at least meet the hiring manager. As a first step, he asked for my CV. At the time, I did not even have one—that's how far-removed corporate life was from my mind.

Days passed, and I continued to put off sending my CV. Eventually, my editor called again, this time with urgency.

'Today's the last day. If you don't send it, they'll move on to other candidates,' he said. At that time, I was staying at Malviya Nagar and I had no computer at home, so I hastily wrote my CV by hand. Then I rushed to a neighbourhood PCO, a public call centre that doubled as a fax and photocopy shop. The shop owner, Pankaj, helped me send the fax to PepsiCo's Gurgaon office. I later learnt that the person reviewing my application edited the handwritten version before having it typed on the computer and processed in their internal system.

After several rounds of interviews, including with HR and department heads, I had the opportunity to meet the legendary Priya Mohan Sinha, fondly called Suman by everyone. Suman had earned a formidable reputation as a business leader from his days at Hindustan Unilever and then at the helm of PepsiCo India, and it was rare for him to interview managerial candidates, but given his belief in the importance of corporate communications, he made an exception. When the call finally came, I was informed that I had been selected but would be given the position of a 'media consultant' as the hiring freeze was still in place. And then I sat on the decision for weeks, unsure whether to leave journalism. Eventually, my editor called me again, urging me to decide. His advice was simple—'Go home, sleep over it and don't ask too many people for advice. It will only make you more confused.'

The next day, I returned to my editor. His reassurance sealed it for me. 'If you don't like it, the doors at PTI will be open for you for as long as I am here,' he said. With that safety net, I accepted the offer. Ironically, three months later, my editor himself left PTI to become a communications consultant with DuPont. Life has funny ways of turning things around.

So, I joined PepsiCo almost at the turn of the century, and more importantly, at the height of a raging cola-war.

Needless to say, it was the proverbial 'baptism by fire'. Moving from a lively and thriving newsroom environment at PTI to a multinational corporation was a cultural shift, and the transition was anything but easy.

In March 2000, just three months into the new millenium, I moved to Gurgaon, which was then more like a distant outpost of the national capital, leaving behind the lively middle-class community of Malviya Nagar in Delhi.

The initial months were challenging. Fortunately, I had an exceptional mentor in my boss Deepak Jolly, a stalwart in the communication fraternity. Deepak provided me with tremendous freedom and taught me the nuances of corporate communication and PR. PepsiCo itself had a remarkable culture—empowering, supportive and deeply professional.

I remember feeling a sense of immense pride seeing my business card carrying the PepsiCo logo and the title 'Media Consultant'. Coming from a small town in Odisha to Delhi to become a journalist, and now working for a global brand in less than five years of working at the national capital—it felt like I had achieved something significant. Six months later, I officially joined the company as a corporate communication manager.

A significant experience was managing the external environment and the public perception about the industry. At the time, soft drinks were often seen as frivolous, non-essential products. The excise duty on carbonated soft drinks (CSDs) was disproportionately high, comparable to luxury items like yachts and even higher than tobacco. This reflected a lack of understanding among key stakeholders about the industry.

Our challenge was to change this perception. That was my first exposure to a serious advocacy campaign. Through a well-thought-out outreach initiative, we strategically engaged with all the key stakeholders, including senior media professionals and policymakers, to highlight the industry's role in generating employment and contributing to the government exchequer. Our proactive advocacy succeeded in bringing into the narrative a sharp focus on how reducing excise duties would lead to lower prices, driving up consumption, increasing sales volumes and, ultimately, boosting tax revenues.

At a time when strategic advocacy was still at a nascent stage, this particular initiative became a benchmark in the profession. On the reactive side, I faced one of the most challenging crises during my time at PepsiCo—which has come to be known as the 'pesticide controversy'. Allegations of high percentage of pesticide residues in soft drinks came from a credible organisation and led to a wave of consumer protests and boycott of the products of both PepsiCo and Coca-Cola. It also resulted in intense media scrutiny, leading to the central government setting up a Joint Parliamentary Committee (JPC) to probe the matter.

Managing this crisis required swift, measured and credible responses, supported by empirical data. Consumers needed assurance that what they were drinking was safe. We collaborated with health experts, regulators and global organisations to present factual, science-based evidence. Studies confirmed that pesticide levels in soft drinks were far below permissible limits, often lower than residues found in commonly consumed fruits and vegetables.

While the crisis was undoubtedly challenging, it was also a tremendous learning experience. Navigating public scrutiny, managing stakeholder relationships and maintaining brand credibility in such highly volatile situations gave me invaluable insights into crisis management and the power of strategic communication.

Overall, my six years at PepsiCo were a period of immense growth and learning. The challenges I faced, both competitive and operational, prepared me for the dynamic landscape of corporate communications, equipping me with skills that have stayed with me throughout my career. PepsiCo was more than just a workplace. The relationships I built there have lasted a lifetime. Many colleagues remain close friends and mentors. The connection goes beyond professional ties, and we still celebrate each other's successes.

Around the end of 2004, I received a call for an opportunity with the erstwhile Hero Honda, now Hero MotoCorp, to set-up its corporate communication function. I went through the interview process, meeting their legendary chairman, Brijmohan Lall Munjal, and Pawan Munjal, who was the CEO at that time. Two key factors influenced my decision to make the switch. First, the opportunity to build something new in a legacy organisation like Hero was rare. Second, the role was a significant step up in terms of responsibility for me. Also, I would be reporting directly to the top leadership. It was an exciting proposition.

In March 2005, I joined Hero Honda. It was a period of immense learning and professional growth. The company's culture, leadership and commitment to innovation made it an extraordinary experience. In August 2024, after almost twenty years with Hero MotoCorp, I transitioned to JSW Group. It was not an easy decision, but the opportunity to join one of the fastest-growing conglomerates in the country was compelling. Working under the inspiring leadership of Sajjan Jindal and his son Parth, who passionately leads the sports vertical in addition to cement, paints, defence, auto and the B2B businesses, has been a new chapter of growth and challenge.

A lot of folks have been talking about the VUCA world for a long time, and I don't think we are out of it yet! With the world continuing to face increasing volatility, uncertainty, complexity and ambiguity, there is a huge opportunity for communicators to play the role of catalysts of change and make a difference to the world.

## 23

# Manish Kalghatgi

### Former Head - Corporate Communications, L&T

---

*'We first make our habits. Then our habits make us.'*

I WAS BORN AND RAISED IN MUMBAI. MY FATHER HAD A BANK job with the Union Bank of India and my mother was a homemaker. Since my father had a transferrable job, I studied in four different schools and three different colleges across India.

My eventual foray into public relations can be blamed on the habits I had unintentionally cultivated in my growing years. While never a topper in studies, I was consistently in the top ten percentile of my class through the school years. However, I never developed a visceral liking for any of my school subjects that would want me pursue any of them into a career path. What I had unknowingly, and without anyone nudging me, developed was a habit of regularly consuming news content. In small town India of the 1970s and early 1980s, that essentially meant reading newspapers and listening to radio (television came in the mid-1980s). Right from my early teens I would read one newspaper daily and listen to BBC Radio on most evenings. Over the years, this habit grew (with access to resources such as the British Library, etc.) and resulted in developing within me not just an awareness of issues but also a perspective on them.

Eventually, after graduating in geology, I decided to change track and ventured into a post-graduation in communication and journalism. That would lead to a five-year stint as a journalist at the beginning of my career, before I made the shift to PR.

Ask any kids of the 1970s who have grown up on the staple diet of Hindi films, and they will instantly resonate with the term Silver Jubilee (twenty-five weeks). It is the recognition of a film's resounding audience acceptance leading to unquestionable box office success, much like a rocket that only goes higher and higher amidst cheers and applause. On the other hand, a Silver Jubilee (twenty-five years) in PR is more of battle of attrition, a continuous ebb and flow, comprising crests of well-planned and well executed campaigns with some troughs of challenging situations.

In my thirty years in the profession, I have criss-crossed the aisle a few times to go from the consulting side into an in-house corporate communications role and vice versa. Starting off as a client servicing executive at a PR consultancy where the day began looking for client mentions in the morning newspapers to becoming the head of corporate communications of a conglomerate, where you plan and craft the messages that the company management should convey to stakeholders, I have had the good fortune of playing a part in landmark issues and events that corporate India has witnessed across sectors in that time.

From planning and executing market introduction of ultra-luxury automobiles, to being stationed in a foreign country for half a year to set right an acquisition process gone messy, from being at the forefront of the strategic repositioning of a blue-chip conglomerate to handling a 'crisis room' for sixty hours non-stop in the aftermath of a major global terrorism event, my voyage in the profession of PR has been eventful and memorable.

Along the way, I endeavoured to develop some personal traits that I felt were vital in performing my role, especially in senior positions. Some of these are:

a. *Curiosity about the world*: This existed due to my early habits.
b. *Active listening*: Mind you, listening is also communication. When you listen well, you better understand the context of what and how to respond.
c. *Adaptability*: The profession constantly throws challenges at you. Those who can adapt well tend to thrive and enjoy the ride.
d. *Trustworthiness and dependability*: As you grow in the profession, you deal with sensitive information and are asked to give advice on critical issues.
e. *Patience and empathy*: A PR professional is essentially an ambassador who has to interact with varied stakeholders, some of whom may not always be favourably inclined to the organisation you represent.

# 24

# Himanshu Kapadia

## HEAD - CORPORATE COMMUNICATIONS, GRASIM INDUSTRIES LIMITED

*'I have truly enjoyed my journey, and I have no regrets.'*

I WAS BORN IN MUMBAI IN 1971. WE COME FROM HUMBLE beginnings, and I can recall the tough times, not for me but for my parents. My dad's business was in textiles, and we were often bankrupt. At that time, we lived in Kalbadevi, the heart of the textile trade. My father had very little money after the joint family split. The choice was either to move to Borivali, a predominantly Gujarati area, or to a notorious neighbourhood, Cuffe Parade, which was primarily Anglo-Indian. Despite warnings, my dad decided to buy a house in Cuffe Parade, not wanting to travel by train. I was only four, and my brother was two. God has been kind, and I often reflect on how that was a brilliant investment.

My father always thought I'd become a chartered accountant, but my true passion was the Air Force. I was an active NCC cadet in school and later in college, even earning a student pilot licence. However, I failed the height-weight ratio test for the Air Force in Class 12, which really saddened my father. After failing my Air Force entrance test, my father suggested I get into the stock market. I joined GG Shine Company, which marked the beginning of my real growth.

I got involved in jobbing, working in the stock exchange rings, learning about shares and mutual funds. I remember the influence of people like Manu Manek, whose presence in the market commanded respect. I got interested in mutual funds and IPOs, which led me to a job with Concept Communications. It was through a connection with Vivek Suchanti's father, Nirmal Suchanti, that I began working in the advertising and PR field. My initial salary was a modest ₹2,000, but that was just the start. I worked in every role possible, from peon to cleaner, doing everything from accounts to PR to advertising.

In 1995, I got engaged. During that time, I also enrolled in an evening diploma programme in marketing from Jamnalal Bajaj Institute, as I had always regretted not pursuing an MBA. However, I got so caught up in work—particularly with all the IPOs and other business opportunities—that I missed the test. I still remember wanting to go for it, but Vivek advised me to wait until the next year, which is how I never ended up taking the exam, although I completed the course.

Throughout this period, I closely observed Madan Bahal and Rajesh Chaturvedi, both of whom I found to be magnetic personalities with a certain aura. Another person I admired was Sunil Gautam, who was known for his stylish presence, much like Rajesh.

I started my journey as the youngest CEO at age twenty-five at Concept, a milestone that I hold dear. Ashish Jalan was a part of our organisation. Vivek, always looking for new investment opportunities, once invested in a film company with Ketan Mehta, known for the special effects studio Maya the Magic Shop. Ashish, a college friend of Vivek's, joined this venture later and became involved in the movie business, which was a passion project for Vivek. Together, they worked on a film called *Jodi Kya Banayi Wah Ramji*, where I even made a cameo appearance alongside Paresh Rawal. It was a fun experience, but the film business ultimately resulted in significant losses. After this episode in the film industry, Ashish decided to return to his business roots. Vivek encouraged him to join Concept PR, and as I was looking to expand my team, I welcomed the idea. Ashish joined Concept PR in 2005, and we worked on several major accounts, including Birla Group and Malaysia Tourism.

In terms of operations, Vivek primarily managed the business side, while I focused on the day-to-day operations and P&L. However, in 2005, I began feeling stagnated. I felt like I was always going to be seen as just a friend within the organisation. After a period of reflection, I reached out to Madan Bahal for advice. I shared my feelings of stagnation with him, and he suggested I join Adfactors PR. I was ready for the change, but I also knew it would be difficult since Vivek was like family to me, and I was joining hands with the competition.

I set three conditions for my potential transition. First, I would not take any clients from Concept PR. Second, I would not share any internal knowledge about Concept PR with Adfactors PR, as I had been involved in everything. And third, I would not bring anyone from Concept PR to Adfactors PR. Madan agreed to these terms. After a difficult conversation with Vivek where he was very understanding, a smooth transition took place. I brought in B.N. Kumar, a close friend who had previously worked at Ogilvy and *Business India*. I offered him the role of CEO, with full autonomy, while Vivek remained the owner.

I spent five years at Adfactors PR. One day, the legendary Pragnya Ram asked me, 'Why don't you join us? You're young, what's your career path?' That question really made me stop and think. I had spent fourteen years in education — from school to my professional courses. Perhaps it was time to shift focus, step into the corporate world and align myself with the values of Birla. Birla, with its legacy, has always held a special place in my heart. I still remember when Aditya Birla visited my college, and my brother, who held the Birla, Tata and Ambani families in high regard, was blessed by him. I feel incredibly blessed to have these connections, which have guided me throughout my career.

I have always believed in living in the present. If you do things right now, the next moment will unfold. Keep focusing on the present because the future takes care of itself. If you keep dwelling on the future, you miss out on the value of today. This moment is what matters.

# 25

# Sanjiv Kataria

**FORMER GROUP EXECUTIVE VICE PRESIDENT - MARKETING COMMUNICATIONS, NIIT & NIIT TECHNOLOGIES**

―――

*'I'm proud of the work I've done in establishing several brands—leveraging strong media relationships.'*

I WAS BORN IN PATIALA IN 1955. MY FATHER WAS A BANKER and my mother an academic. I have only faint memories of my early childhood in Patiala. My more vivid recollections begin around age seven or eight, when my father was transferred to Yamunanagar, now in Haryana. That's where my real childhood began—in a townhouse with a large garden and a vast mango grove nearby. I still remember the delight of eating mangoes straight from the trees. I also recall the death of Jawaharlal Nehru, nights spent in trenches during the 1965 Indo–Pak war and growing up with *The Tribune*.

We returned to Patiala for two years, during which I attended Modern School. My father's next posting was to

Khanna, where I completed my schooling. Another transfer took us to Jalandhar, where I joined DAV College for an undergraduate degree. I was actively involved with the college magazine's editorial team, and it was here that my interest in reading, writing and public speaking truly developed.

After graduating in 1975, I secured admission to the Department of Journalism at Panjab University, Chandigarh. Those were among my best academic years. I was also nominated to the University Students' Council, a unique privilege during the Emergency, when elections were suspended.

Fresh out of journalism school in 1976, I began my career at DCM Chemical Works as a communications officer, producing a monthly house journal and managing internal communications for the DCM Shriram Group. Those five years at DCM gave me a ringside view of the world of public relations. My boss also managed the group's flagship events—the DCM Football Tournament and the Shankar Shad Mushaira. I occasionally sat in on media briefings, including one memorable session when complaints of gas emissions brought *Hindustan Times*' chief reporter, Prabha Dutt (a senior alum from Chandigarh), to the factory.

In 1981, I joined the India Tourism Development Corporation (ITDC) as manager—publicity planning in its Marketing Communications Division. It was an exciting time for Indian tourism, especially with the 1982 Asian Games driving the development of new properties, including three by ITDC—Samrat, Kanishka and Ashok Yatri Niwas. I was responsible for publicity and promotion for several state tourism departments.

A major portion of my work involved integrated marketing communications for Jammu & Kashmir Tourism, under a very demanding Director Mohiuddin Shah. I also handled assignments from the tourism boards of Odisha, Rajasthan, Gujarat and Madhya Pradesh.

A pivotal experience was leading ITDC's communications task force for the 1986 National Cultural Festival. I saw how non-traditional media—art, culture and music at heritage sites—could serve as a powerful medium for national integration. That experience strengthened my belief in communications as a tool for public good, not just for promotion.

At ITDC, I had the privilege of working under media and marketing stalwarts like Anees Jung (former editor of *Youth Times*, for whom I had written during my college days), PR guru Rabindra Seth (who taught me the power of concise communication, having been trained as a Second World War radio reporter) and VP Marketing Ranjana Khanna, who inspired me to pursue an Executive MBA at FMS, Delhi.

In September 1987, I joined NIIT as advertising manager, working closely with founder Rajendra S. Pawar, my mentor in marketing and communications. My role quickly expanded to include direct marketing, brand building and employee engagement. A media crisis in 1989 pushed me into the PR frontlines.

A PTI newswire incorrectly reported that NIIT—then known as the National Institute of Information Technology—had been ordered to shut down. The actual issue was a directive from the Monopolies and Restrictive Trade Practices Commission (MRTPC) to stop advertising a '100% placement guarantee', despite our strong record. But the misinformation spiralled. All India Radio picked up the report and broadcast it in multiple languages, sparking panic among our franchisees.

That episode was a baptism by fire. Guided by PR veteran Sat Saraf, I met news editors at *The Economic Times* and *The Times of India*, who corrected the record. A tense meeting with Doordarshan's news director nearly led to the story airing again—until we clarified our position and the story was withdrawn. It taught me my first key lesson in PR: never let legal language overtake the human narrative. Clarity, humility and access to editors matter more.

From that point on, PR became integral to my role. We worked to transform NIIT's reputation from a coaching centre into a credible national institution, highlighting stories of students from modest backgrounds who returned to recruit others after finding success. We launched 'Meet the Press' sessions across cities. Workshops like 'The Role of Computers in Mass Communication' in the late 1980s and early 1990s, introducing the medium to journalists, well ahead of the digital revolution, were gamechangers. Watching editors like Usha Rai, Bobby Ghosh and Rajendra Prabhu embrace computers was immensely rewarding.

During the early-2000s dot-com bust, when enrolments dropped and NIIT posted its first-ever losses, we launched a transparent educational PR campaign. I personally met over a hundred editors to explain why this was the right time to invest in IT training. Real-life stories of transformation, especially through our GNIIT programme and the rollout of over 1,000 classrooms in government schools in Andhra Pradesh and Karnataka, underpinned our message.

One of our most impactful campaigns came in 2002, when we launched World Computer Literacy Day (WCLD) on NIIT's twentieth Foundation Day. Designed to train 100,000 people in a single day, it included the SWIFT Jyoti programme and later evolved to focus on women's digital empowerment.

The campaign reached unexpected quarters—the inmates of Tihar Jail, the West Bengal Assembly for legislators, the Parliament House Annexe for parliamentarians cheered on by

Prime Minister Vajpayee. It was PR with purpose, anchored in education, aspiration and empowerment.

We also partnered with media houses to amplify WCLD outreach, and later engaged IPAN and TBWA Anthem PR to shape NIIT's GNIIT branding and engagement with world chess champion Viswanathan Anand. The NIIT MindChampions' Academy demonstrated his picture-perfect memory through simultaneous chess sessions with groups of students, celebrities and even soldiers recovering from the Kargil War at the Army Hospital.

We empowered our franchisees with standardised messaging, media kits and story frameworks, building a decentralised yet cohesive PR engine well before 'brand consistency' became a buzzword.

Looking back, our strength lay in consistently delivering best-in-class products, benchmarked services and lifelong engagement. Our media relationships were built on a promise: NIIT would tell authentic stories—always with empathy, honesty and purpose.

We understood that great communication is about building lasting trust. And remembering that every journalist we engaged with wasn't just a messenger, but a potential ally in shaping public understanding.

As I approached my fiftieth birthday in 2005, I discussed the next chapter of my professional journey with Mr Pawar. My formal exit from NIIT in 2008 marked the beginning of a new phase focused on reputation management and purposeful storytelling. Through a boutique consultancy, I set out to help CEOs communicate clearly and directly with the media, drawing on decades of trusted editorial relationships.

Post-NIIT, I consulted for global brands such as Encyclopaedia Britannica, IDC, Pearson VUE,

Teleperformance, UNSW and the Vienna Tourist Board, as well as home-grown names like CyberMedia, Vee Technologies, the Sona Education Institutions and Webdunia. Supporting start-ups backed by IAN, VentureNursery and Techstars brought fresh and engaging brand-building opportunities.

It's been a fulfilling journey—anchored in the belief that honest communication makes all the difference.

# 26

# Raza Khan

## Head - PR & Communications, udaan

―⚍―

*'If there's one key takeaway from my experience, it is this: read extensively. Absorb news, analyse it critically and apply that knowledge to enhance your work.'*

I was born in Jagdalpur, the district headquarters of Bastar in Chhattisgarh. While Bastar is often associated with Naxalite-related news, the cities, including Jagdalpur, remain largely unaffected. I spent my childhood there and completed my schooling at Nirmal Vidyalaya before moving to Raipur for higher education.

My father was a branch manager at the Union Bank of India, and my mother, who initially worked as a teacher, later became a homemaker. Due to my father's transferable job, we moved frequently within towns of Madhya Pradesh, which later became part of the newly carved state of Chhattisgarh. Eventually, we settled in Jagdalpur, where I completed my schooling before heading to NIT Raipur for my graduation.

In the 1990s, career choices were largely limited to engineering or medical sciences. Since I excelled in mathematics and science, I cleared the PET (Pre-Engineering Test) in my first attempt and pursued B.E. in Chemical Engineering from NIT, Raipur.

After graduation, I was placed at Lupin Laboratories in Bhopal, working as a chemical engineer at their Mandideep plant. However, within six months, I realised that factory life was not for me. Coming from a middle-class family, I discussed my dilemma with my parents. They gave me two options: either pursue higher studies or find another job, but returning home to prepare for further exams was not an option.

Determined to transition into a different field, I attempted the Management Aptitude Test (MAT) and set out on a new career path. I got into the Delhi School of Communication (DSC) in Delhi, choosing it over three or four other options. What set it apart was its unique PG Diploma in Communication, which covered marketing, public relations, advertising, market research and journalism. This was in 1996, when most postgraduate programmes focused only on three mainstream MBA specialisations—marketing, HR or finance. Seeing the diverse curriculum at DSC, I knew it was an option worth exploring.

My most significant internship was with Mudra, an advertising agency, where I worked in media planning, leveraging my strength in mathematics and analytics. I stayed there for nearly a year, and they appreciated my work. I was keen on pursuing a career in media planning, but unfortunately, there were no job openings at Mudra at that time.

I started exploring other opportunities and landed an entry level role at Perfect Relations. Though my initial preference was to work in advertising, particularly in media planning, that was not to be. I found my way into the PR profession and began my journey at Perfect Relations.

In the beginning, the work was extremely challenging. Back then, there was no online media tracking, no measurement tools and no automated systems. Regardless of the season—monsoon, summer or winter—we had to be in the office by 4.30 or 5 a.m. Our job was to manually scan newspapers for client coverage, cut out relevant clippings, paste them onto sheets and create photocopied dockets. A few runners in the office would then deliver these reports to clients by 8.30 or 9 a.m.

This process instilled the habit of reading newspapers thoroughly and staying updated on industry developments. Today, it's almost unimaginable. If you tell young professionals about manually tracking newspapers, they'd think it was a waste of time. But back then, there was no option and this was how media tracking was done. These early challenges and learnings strengthened the foundation of our career in PR.

A unique pattern played a vital role in my career—every few months, one of my reporting bosses would leave the organisation. Since I was performing well, I kept getting promoted to fill the gaps. If an associate manager left, I was made an associate manager on the condition that I performed. Then the manager would leave, and I'd move up again. In just three-and-a-half years, I found myself heading the Delhi branch of Perfect Relations.

This was both the most challenging and rewarding phase of my career, as I reported directly to the founders, Dilip Cherian and Bobby Kewalramani. Learning from these pioneers was intense but invaluable. It was a tough training ground, but it shaped my entire approach to PR.

After spending seven years at Perfect Relations, I decided to take the next step in my career. At the time, Genesis PR (now

Burson) was considered the finishing school of PR, known for honing strategic thinking, client management and presentation skills. Genesis was known for these strengths, making it the ideal place to refine my skills.

At Genesis, I led the Consumer and Entertainment practice, handling brands like the National Dairy Development Board (NDDB), Mother Dairy, BBC, National Geographic and the History Channel.

After exactly one year at Genesis, I received an offer from one of India's finest corporate houses, Bharti. The person leading communications at Bharti, Senjam Raj Sekhar, was also a former employee of Genesis. So instead of a formal interview, we had a general discussion about Genesis, Perfect Relations and the telecom industry. Before I knew it, I had an offer from Bharti.

The cherry on the cake at Bharti was working directly with a business icon, one of the tallest leaders globally and, I dare say, the leader with the finest understanding of public relations in the country, Sunil Bharti Mittal. Working with Mittal was one of the best learning experiences I had in my PR career.

My time at Bharti spanned fourteen years, covering pivotal moments in India's telecom landscape.

In 2006, I joined Bharti and worked there until 2020, except for a brief one-year stint at Tata Quippo (later known as Viom Infrastructure), a Tata Group joint venture that provided telecom towers to service providers. I joined Viom as the head of communications but was called back to Bharti when Senjam resigned from Bharti.

By 2020, I felt it was time for a new challenge. After fourteen years in telecom and corporate communications, I started exploring other options. E-commerce was booming. That's when I got an offer from udaan, a company looking for a communications leader with experience in public markets.

This new role allowed me to broaden my expertise beyond telecom and into the ever-dynamic e-commerce sector. Today, at udaan, I lead the entire communications portfolio—corporate storytelling, social media, external media relations and internal communications.

If there is one key takeaway from my experience, it is this: read extensively. Absorb news, analyse it critically and apply that knowledge to enhance your work—whether you are in a consultancy managing clients or an in-house PR professional shaping your company's reputation.

Equally important in our profession is the ability to think on your feet. The pace of crisis management has drastically changed with social media. A single tweet or post can damage a company's reputation.

What makes this field exciting are the daily challenges, the unpredictability and the impact we create. That's why I have embraced new sectors regularly over the years, always eager to tackle fresh challenges and learn continuously.

# 27

# Alpana Killawala

FORMER PRINCIPAL ADVISOR -
COMMUNICATION, RESERVE BANK OF INDIA

---

*'My professional journey was a constant balancing act, ensuring transparency without compromising on integrity.'*

I AM A TRUE MUMBAIKAR. I WAS BORN, RAISED, EDUCATED IN Mumbai and also worked in the city. My father retired as a regional manager in a general insurance company, while my mother initially started as a schoolteacher before transitioning to social work.

I studied at what is now called Lions High School in Vile Parle East. Our family originally lived in Vile Parle East before moving to Santacruz West. My early education began at Chaitanya Bal Mandir, founded by Chaitanya Ben, who was also our principal. What started as a kindergarten eventually expanded into a full-fledged school, where I completed my schooling. I was fortunate to have great teachers who provided many opportunities for learning and growth.

After completing my bachelor's degree, I was clear that I wanted to start working as I wanted to be financially independent. Initially, I enrolled in a master's programme in political science and psychology, mostly because my friends were pursuing it. Once I completed my studies, I started working at the Indian Banks' Association in the editorial section.

At work, I was fortunate to have two exceptional mentors. My immediate boss, Meena Ranade, played a crucial role in honing my editing and communication skills. She taught me how to refine and sharpen content with precision. The head of the organisation, N.S. Pradhan, had a unique and engaging way of teaching.

One day, Pradhan called me into his office. As I walked in, he remarked, 'Here comes a soldier without his ammunition,' or something to that effect. 'Whenever you meet your boss, even if you have perfect memory, always carry a notepad and pen. It shows that you are paying attention and taking the conversation seriously.' That lesson on perception and professionalism has stayed with me ever since. From that moment on, I never entered a boss's office without a pen and paper.

On another occasion, while approving minutes of a meeting, he remarked, 'Hamlet without the Prince of Denmark.' Though I had studied Shakespeare during my second master's in English, the meaning of his words did not immediately register. Perplexed, I left his office and asked my immediate boss, Ranade, what he meant. When she could not figure it out either, she encouraged me to go back and ask him directly. So I did. He smiled and explained that I had forgotten to mention the chairman's name in the minutes!

That first job at the Indian Banks' Association lasted eight years. By the time I left, I had risen to the position of editor for the journal where I initially worked as manager. I then moved to *Business India* as a reporter, covering banking, finance and the Reserve Bank of India (RBI). Given that RBI was traditionally media-shy, it was challenging for journalists to gain access. However, I managed to build relationships and secure meetings with key figures, including the governor at the time, Venkitaramanan.

He was an open-minded leader, ahead of his time in terms of regulatory transparency and engagement with the press. Interestingly, unknown to me, he had often suggested within the organisation that they needed someone like 'me' in their press division. The team subtly hinted to me at the possibility, but I was too focused on my work at *Business India* to catch on. Eventually, RBI formally advertised the role—being a public institution, they had to follow due process. Some RBI officials encouraged me to apply, but I hesitated. I was thoroughly enjoying my job at *Business India*—meeting people, writing stories and gaining deep insights into the financial world.

Despite my initial reluctance, the opportunity at RBI was too significant to ignore. My father was particularly thrilled—joining a premier institution like RBI was a matter of great pride. Even Ashok Advani encouraged me, saying, 'If you get a chance to work at an institution like RBI, take it. And if you don't like it, you can always come back—once a journalist, always a journalist.' That reassurance gave me the confidence to take the leap.

Once I joined RBI, the stark contrast in work culture was quite apparent. Unlike the flexibility at *Business India*, RBI was a hierarchical institution with a rigid approval process. Everything required formal authorisation, and the institution itself would not make things easier for you—you had to navigate it on your own. Initially, I found the system stifling. But over time, I came to understand the rationale behind it and appreciated it. RBI's rules were designed for consistency—if exceptions were made for one individual, it would create a precedent that others would expect as well. Eventually, I began to appreciate the structure and discipline that came with working in such an institution.

At *Business India*, Ashok Advani had once told me, 'The less you're in the office, the better—because it means you're out meeting people.' At RBI, however, the expectation was a strict 10-to-5 schedule, often extending beyond office hours. It was a shift I had to adapt to, but one that brought its own set of invaluable experiences and learning opportunities.

Despite the gruelling workload, the learning experience was invaluable. I had the privilege of working with six or seven RBI governors. From the outside, journalists and analysts often criticised RBI, claiming it lacked foresight or agility. But having worked within the institution, I saw firsthand the depth of thought behind every decision.

One major milestone was incorporating media advertising—a rare move for central banks globally. Traditionally, central banks communicate through the media rather than through direct advertisements. However, I strongly believed that regulatory messages should reach the public in their original form, without being filtered or reinterpreted by journalists. Since social media and digital platforms were not prevalent at the time, advertising became the most effective way to ensure clarity and direct communication with the public.

Another key initiative was transforming RBI's press releases. Instead of issuing them in RBI's dense, bureaucratic language, I rewrote them in a news-style format that was easier for journalists to understand. This improved media coverage and ensured that the public received clearer, more accurate information.

By 1996, with the emergence of the internet, we were among the first central banks to launch a website. Though I had no background in web technology, I quickly learnt on the job and recognised the website's potential to become our primary communication platform. Today, the RBI website serves as the primary reference point for banking regulations and updates and most of all, data.

Beyond the website, we introduced several other initiatives. We were among the first central banks to formally start training journalists on RBI's functions and working. It was not just an overview—it was an in-depth course on central banking, with experts who wrote the regulations explaining them firsthand.

RBI governors understood and valued communication. Despite institutional resistance to change, they supported my initiatives, enabling transformation. By the time I left after twenty-six years, we had evolved from a basic press relations division into a full-fledged Department of Communication. We even took on advertising, an unusual step for a central bank, launching campaigns like RBI Kehta Hai with Amitabh Bachchan to directly inform the public. The campaign continues to this day, which gives me immense satisfaction.

Demonetisation was a defining chapter in my career—it was actually the last major crisis I handled before leaving RBI. It was an extraordinary experience, but also deeply challenging. This was followed by the pandemic: both events significantly sped up the shift to digital payments. However, by the time the pandemic struck, I had already retired from RBI in 2019.

My time at RBI was an extraordinary learning experience. Every day brought new challenges, both internal—navigating institutional resistance—and external, managing media relations. It was a constant balancing act, ensuring transparency without compromising the institution's integrity.

## 28

# Rakhee Lalvani

### FORMER CHIEF COMMUNICATIONS OFFICER, TAJ HOTELS

*'I believe that leadership is about inclusion—about carrying people with you and being there for them as much as you want them to be there for you.'*

I COME FROM A MIDDLE-CLASS BACKGROUND, WHERE MY mother was a homemaker and my father worked as a company secretary for a few companies. I had a brother, who unfortunately passed away in 2021 in 2021. Though I was born in Calcutta, I moved to Bangalore when I was very young, and I consider myself a Bangalorean. I completed my schooling at Mount Carmel, an all-women's college in Bangalore. In 1989, I decided to take an unconventional route and pursue a career outside of the traditional fields like commerce or science.

I initially aimed to explore arts and architecture, but due to my lack of maths skills, I shifted towards hotel management. It seemed like a glamorous and aspirational industry at the time. My brother guided me, and that's how I ended up in hotel management, joining as a management trainee in the industry. I went on to study at a hotel school in Chennai, and then returned to Bangalore where I was interviewed by top hotel groups like the Oberoi and Taj. I chose the Taj, as my family was particularly keen on the Tatas.

However, after undergoing extensive training and realising the reality of hotel work, I quickly realised that the glamorous facade did not hold up. The work often involved mundane tasks and I did not find hotel operations appealing. My brother suggested I consider sales and marketing instead—a field I knew little about at the time. I took a chance, met the MD and got a break in sales and marketing at Taj.

I initially struggled, feeling out of my depth, being the only non-MBA in a team mostly filled with people with advanced degrees. But I worked hard, putting in long hours, immersing myself in learning and seeking guidance from mentors. Eventually, my boss recognised my potential and entrusted me with more responsibilities, helping me grow in my career. After many years of hard work, I went through what I can call a 'mid-life crisis' at thirty-five, realising that I had been working sixteen to seventeen-hour days without respite. I decided I needed a change.

In the last thirty years, most of my career has been spent working full time with the Indian Hotels Company Limited, and I have had a fulfilling journey within the hospitality industry.

My career trajectory at the Taj was incredible. I began my career as a management trainee and quickly transitioned into pure sales. From there, I became a hotel sales manager, and each role felt like stepping into a new company, as each opportunity brought a completely different set of challenges and responsibilities. As a hotel manager, I was responsible for the P&L, learning to read balance sheets and managing the revenues and profitability of the hotel. In essence, we became the custodians of the business, operating as business owners and managers. This was a stark contrast to sales, where the focus is purely on targets. After that, I had the opportunity to lead the sales and marketing efforts for multiple hotels. Each transition in my career offered a chance to redefine my role. While there were certain aspects laid out in the job description, I always sought to craft my position in a way that allowed me to make a meaningful impact. This drive to excel was always stronger than the desire for change or to work in different companies.

For me, it was not about exploring different sectors or gaining new knowledge—it was about pushing myself to excel in whatever role I took on. I wanted to be the best, to go beyond the expectations of a salesperson or a hotel manager.

When PR came into the picture, it was not something I would have chosen on my own, but the MD saw potential in me. At the time, I was feeling burnt out and in need of change. What really helped me was having great mentors. That kind of leadership, where you're nurtured and supported, is crucial. They did not just let me go; they helped me grow, and that made all the difference in my career.

When I first moved to Mumbai, I really did not like the city. It felt overwhelming—too loud, too chaotic. Being part of the Taj's resurrection after the terror attack of 2008 and managing the crisis post-26/11 became a defining experience for me. It reshaped how I approached crises; nothing ever really felt like a crisis after that. I was not in Taj Bombay during the attacks; I was in Bangalore. My predecessor was caught in one of the outlets during the attacks and could not continue in her role, so I was flown in a couple of days after the incident. I took over the crisis management and helped steer the brand's rebuilding. At that time, the Taj Mahal Palace was synonymous with the Taj brand globally, and rebuilding it became a major focus. This period became a case study for me in crisis management and leadership.

I came to realise that I did not need to be aggressive or pretend to act in a certain way. I'm naturally a people's person, so I embraced that. I focused on being empathetic, honest and transparent with my team. It was important for me to be open with them, even showing vulnerability at times. I have cried in front of my colleagues and bosses, and I have always told them not to worry because I would be fine in a few minutes. This authenticity helped me build stronger relationships and trust within my team. I believe that leadership is about inclusion—about carrying people with you and being there for them as much as you want them to be there for you.

As for advice to younger professionals, especially in PR, I believe the most important thing is maintaining relationships. Despite the digital age and the ease of WhatsApp, the core of PR is still about personal connections. You need to put in the effort to build and nurture those relationships. That relationship capital will always give you the best returns.

PR today requires a broader skill set. It's no longer just about knowing traditional PR; you need to understand digital marketing, influencer marketing, SEO and the entire ecosystem of integrated communications. PR professionals cannot afford to work in isolation anymore—it is all about 360-degree engagement.

However, one thing that has not changed is the need for good, creative content. In today's cluttered world, if you are not differentiated, you will not stand out. You have to understand your audience's pulse and craft your content to connect with them, whether through topicality or purpose-driven messaging. Storytelling remains at the heart of it all. No one's interested in scripted language or flowery press releases. To make an impact, you need to tell a story that resonates.

I have now embarked on a journey as a consultant to select brands and I am enjoying this new phase of my professional life.

# 29

# Nivedeeta Moirangthem

## Country Communication Manager, IKEA India

―⚬―

*'My journey has been filled with the privilege of making mistakes and trying to make things better.'*

I WAS BORN IN MANIPUR. MY PARENTS WERE BOTH educationists and were a big influence on my world view as I was growing up. Growing up in a small town, life revolved around family, close friends and the sense of belonging to a larger family or community. My nuclear family consisted of my two brothers, my parents and me, and while we lived separately, we were very closely connected to our extended family. I am grateful for the freedom I had to make life choices—whether it was education, career, friends or simply how I approached life.

After school, I came to Delhi to pursue higher education. I studied at the University of Delhi and later at the Indian Institute of Mass Communication (IIMC), which marked the beginning of my communications career and my first exposure to the communication business. Right after graduation, I was offered a role at McCann Erickson, a leading advertising agency. I spent four years working with some advertising stalwarts, learning how to build brands. It was intense, exciting and created the base for my professional journey ahead.

My next career move was with the Park Hotels as PR manager. But soon after joining them I found an opportunity to work with IKEA in 2002. It's been twenty-three years, and I still work at IKEA, thoroughly enjoying it!

When I joined IKEA, my role was not specifically in PR. It was more focused on stakeholder engagement. At that time, I worked with the sourcing and supply organisation in India. There was little external communication because we did not have customer-facing stores. It was more internal communication, stakeholder management and handling organisational growth. Initially, my role was more focused on communication campaigns related to supply chain and compliance within the sourcing organisation. This was primarily B2B, working with our supplier partners in India. We had interventions in areas where we were producing IKEA products, such as carpets, and improving the living conditions of women and children in those areas. Through initiatives with organisations like UNICEF, Save the Children and WHO, we built schools and promoted education for the children of those who were working in the factories.

I have had the opportunity to work in various functions such as sustainability and social initiatives and sourcing. Then I moved to IKEA retail in 2014. This gave me the opportunity to be a part of the first retail team of IKEA India and to open retail stores in India. I consider myself fortunate to have worked with great mentors and leaders and to have got the right opportunities at the right time of my career in IKEA, guiding me at pivotal moments and helping me make the right decisions.

The period between 2002 and 2012 in the sourcing organisation was when my work with the IKEA supply chain had a great impact on me, working with social and environmental norms, code of conduct at factories, local communities, suppliers and artisans, especially in the carpet belt.

The Hyderabad store launch was a major success, not just commercially but in terms of creating awareness and curiosity about the brand. We had already laid a strong foundation, building trust with both customers and stakeholders. However, beyond the numbers, we were even more proud of the relationships we built with society. These connections were crucial as we expanded to Mumbai and Bangalore and now in Delhi and North India.

IKEA's values and culture have always resonated with me and my values and beliefs. And all along, I have had supportive leaders who also challenged me to do better and grow closer to IKEA's values. What stands out is the freedom and accountability that I had all along. Here, you can create your own path. You also have the privilege of making mistakes, testing and trying to make things better. I feel grateful for the company's belief in me, and that has kept me in IKEA for this long.

Today, I am the head of communications and work as part of the IKEA India management team, co-creating the next phase of IKEA's growth journey in India with my colleagues. My core areas of work include both internal and external communication—public affairs, public relations, co-worker communication and transformation communication.

# 30

# Subhayu Mishra

### Managing Director & Head - Global Public Affairs, Citi India

---

*'The importance of reading a newspaper thoroughly, engaging deeply with books and reflecting on what I read—an invaluable lesson that has stayed with me.'*

I AM AN ONLY CHILD. MY MOTHER IS A DOCTOR AND MY father, after a career in government service, transitioned into politics and public life. I grew up in Bhubaneswar, the capital of Odisha, where I completed my schooling and college education. Initially studying science, I later shifted to economics, eventually earning a master's degree before entering the capital markets sector.

My father was a significant influence on my life, particularly in shaping my love for reading and writing. He was an avid reader, consuming four English newspapers and three regional newspapers daily. He would guide me on what to read, encouraging me to analyse news articles and share my understanding. Our home had a rich library, including books, magazines and journals, and he would often recommend a reading list. This exposure to external perspectives shaped my inclination towards outward-facing roles.

Beyond reading, he instilled in me the habit of writing. Whenever we travelled, he would ask me to document my experiences—not necessarily in a grand or literary manner, but simply to structure my thoughts and memories. This practice nurtured my ability to articulate ideas clearly.

I was drawn to research. However, I had a strong interest in marketing, particularly in how psychology is leveraged within it. Communication, as a structured discipline, was not my first choice. If I had followed my initial inclination, I might have pursued research or economics. However, writing, as a core component of communication, was always a part of me.

My career began at Stockholding Corporation of India (SHCIL) in capital markets, but within a few years, I transitioned to the marketing team when the company expanded into retail, offering depository participant services at the onset of dematerialisation.

As part of this shift, I single-handedly managed advertising and PR since we did not have a PR consultancy at the time. My CEO encouraged me to build direct relationships with journalists and understand media dynamics first-hand. This was a steep yet invaluable learning experience. With just one team member, I handled marketing and communications, helping establish the company's credibility as it expanded from a handful of locations to nearly a hundred, many in previously untapped markets.

After six years in this role, I moved in 2005 to the commodities futures exchange sector, recognising its potential as an emerging market. I joined Financial Technologies (India) and led a team focused on brand-building and positioning the commodity futures exchange MCX as a technologically advanced and globally competitive platform for price discovery. A key part of our work involved differentiating MCX from competitors and aligning it with global commodity futures exchanges like the London Metal Exchange. Additionally, I played a role in creating brand identities for subsidiary companies within the Financial Technologies Group, which aimed to build an integrated financial ecosystem.

Despite the exciting work, my tenure at MCX was brief—about a year—before an unexpected opportunity at Chlorophyll, a brand consulting firm. While initially engaged in brand-building discussions for MCX's IPO, I was offered a role in account planning. Though the experience was enriching, I realised I preferred structured, large-scale organisations over consulting, leading me to shift—this time to AIG.

At AIG, I handled external communications for the group while also managing channel marketing and communications for Tata AIG Life Insurance (now Tata AIA Life). This period, from mid-2007 onwards, was one of my most fulfilling corporate experiences. This expansion required extensive engagement with regional media, leveraging the Tata brand's reputation to build credibility and trust—both crucial in the insurance sector.

This was an exciting and transformative period, but as the AIG crisis unfolded due to the subprime mortgage crisis in 2008, it became evident that the scale and ambition of the business would likely be constrained in the short to medium term. Around this time, I received an interesting offer from Barclays—my first opportunity in the banking sector.

Until then, my experience had been in financial services, capital markets, insurance and commodities, but not banking. So, in the winter of 2010, I joined Barclays as the head of communications, CSR and brand for India. Unlike my previous roles, Barclays was a smaller operation, but it had an exceptionally strong investment banking team that consistently delivered outstanding performance. My time at Barclays was a period of immense learning.

My experiences have reinforced the importance of staying composed under pressure, sticking to the narrative and never shying away from media engagement, especially in times of crisis.

In 2012, after two years at Barclays, I joined Standard Chartered, where I spent nearly a decade. One of the key priorities was shaping the right narrative for the organisation, especially as it faced perception issues related to NPAs (non-performing assets).

Thereafter I joined Citi in 2022. The organisation had already announced the divestiture of its consumer banking business in 2021. Just days before I started, Citi announced the sale to Axis Bank. This marked a major shift for Citi in India, as consumer banking had long been the most visible part of the brand.

At Citi, my initial focus was to shape the narrative around this transition. The first priority was to clarify that the decision was part of Citi's global strategy and not a reflection of its commitment to India. Whenever a foreign bank sells off a business, speculation often arises about a potential exit from the country. However, in reality, seldom have foreign banks exited India.

Looking back, I may have been somewhat conservative in my career choices. Start-ups, for example, could have presented high-risk, high-reward scenarios. However, the financial sector's complexity—particularly in regulation and products—has always interested me. Unlike sectors with simpler narratives, this sector requires deeper understanding.

My natural inclination towards research, data analysis and strategic thinking has made a communications career in the financial sector work well, even if I did not plan to stay in this sector. In many ways, the sector chose me as much as I chose it.

# 31

# Rachana Panda

## VP & Head - Cluster Communications, Bayer, ASEAN, ANZ & South Asia

---

*'My approach is simple: focus on doing the work first, build credibility within the system and prove yourself—everything else will follow.'*

I WAS BORN IN DELHI, BUT I SPENT MY SCHOOL YEARS IN Assam, where my father worked at a British tea company and my mother was an academic. Education was a strong value in our household, which led me to pursue a bachelor's degree in science and later, a master's in business administration. I also completed the Advanced Management Program (AMP) at Harvard, which became a pivotal moment in shaping my career and business perspective.

I began my career at Apollo Tyres as a management trainee, a role that introduced me to corporate life. It was here that I met Venkat Ramani, a well-known communicator in the company. His passion for communications intrigued me, and what began as curiosity soon evolved into a lifelong commitment to the field. I quickly realised that effective communication is not just about sharing information—it's about building connections and driving change.

Eager to broaden my experience, I transitioned into the development sector, where I worked on British Council-funded projects in India. It was a highly unconventional role involving project monitoring and collaboration with state governments, NGOs and funders. However, the pull of corporate life remained strong, and I soon found myself leading the communications division at Transport Corporation of India thanks to a referral. This role enhanced my editorial and content skills.

My next significant role was at Alcatel during the telecom boom. It was exciting to work in a rapidly growing sector as we worked on emerging technologies like CDMA and GSM. At Alcatel, I initiated internal communications in the South Asia region and led the launch of Alcatel handsets in Bangladesh and many industry partnerships. The pace was fast and the learning immense.

After Alcatel, I joined Alstom, where I had the opportunity to work across infrastructure sectors like power and rail transportation, thus broadening my experience in large-scale communications. However, it was my time at General Electric as the chief communications and brand officer in the South Asia region that truly defined my approach to communications as a strategic business function. Working under excellent leaders like John Flannery, I saw first-hand how deeply communications could be integrated with the business. It was not just about messaging; it was about ensuring communications had a voice in the decision-making process.

My fascinating journey then brought me to Bayer, in the health and nutrition sector. My time here since 2020 has been quite purposeful and fulfilling. Working at a company with the mission 'Health for all, hunger for none' has deepened my passion for the impact of the work we do.

Bayer's reach is vast, touching lives across different geographies and communities. The organisation recently went through a transformation, which has broadened my communications responsibilities to include ASEAN and ANZ regions along with South Asia. The most exciting part of my role is the opportunity to engage with a wide spectrum of stakeholders—policymakers, communities, women, farmers and other diverse groups. This diversity brings richness to the work, allowing me and my team to tailor communication strategies that resonate deeply with each group. At Bayer, every campaign or communication we design contributes to a larger purpose, whether it's improving access to healthcare, supporting sustainable farming or empowering communities. Our work goes beyond corporate goals, making this journey rewarding.

I would like to share few remarkable campaigns I have been involved with:

a. *Run Blue*: Bayer joined forces with Mina Guli, a renowned ultra-marathon runner, for the Run Blue campaign aimed at raising awareness about water conservation, especially in regions grappling with severe water depletion. The India chapter comprised multiple marathons across India, in Delhi-NCR, Varanasi, Thane and Mumbai. Various stakeholders from the government, farmers, NGOs, associates and employees embraced the cause with enthusiasm, participating in the marathons. The inaugural run in New Delhi was flagged off by Amitabh Kant, India's G-20 Sherpa and former chairman of NITI Aayog. There was substantial traction from the media, leading to coverage across the nation, creating an impact that ignited vibrant discussions on social media platforms. The successful campaign was a testimony of collaboration across Bayer, showcasing our dedication to addressing the critical global water challenge.

b. *125 Years of Bayer in India*: One of the most memorable campaigns I had the privilege to lead was the 125th anniversary of Bayer in India, marking a major milestone in the company's history. This campaign was special not only because of the scale, involving nearly 5,000 employees, associates and partners, but because it gave us a platform to truly showcase our rich legacy. Being one of the first multinational companies to establish a base in India, Bayer has a notable presence, but we had never told our story—until this moment. Amidst the global pandemic, when agriculture and healthcare were in the spotlight, we seized the opportunity to connect both internally and externally in ways we had not before. The campaign resonated deeply with all Bayerites; even their families gathered to watch the virtual event. Externally, the response was equally powerful with the acknowledgment of the steadfast presence in the country. This campaign did not just strengthen brand reputation; it cemented a sense of belonging and pride for everyone involved.

One does not always need to have a detailed plan—I am happy to let things flow naturally. Whatever I do, though, I aim to make a meaningful impact. My approach is simple: focus on doing the work first, build credibility within the system, and prove yourself; everything else will follow.

If I could offer one piece of advice to young professionals, it would be this: practise humility and candidness. These qualities have been my guiding principles, shaping both my career and personal growth.

On a personal note, my greatest joy comes from spending time with my husband and daughter, particularly on our travels. Looking ahead, I hope to dedicate my time to working with children in need, particularly street children.

# 32

# Sujit Patil

## CHIEF COMMUNICATIONS OFFICER, GODREJ INDUSTRIES GROUP

---

*'My professional journey has been a blend of serendipity, passion, curiosity, initiative, recognition and holistic growth.'*

I AM MY PARENTS' FIRST-BORN. MY DAD, MANOHAR PATIL, now a retired scientist from the Bhabha Atomic Research Centre (BARC), was probably hoping to discover the secret of raising a genius. My mom, Meena, now a retired school principal, was there to make sure I did not turn into a total disaster.

Back in the day, career choices were as thrilling as a bowl of plain rice: engineering or medicine. I bravely opted for the former and graduated in instrumentation engineering from Pune University, despite my heart secretly singing 'I Want to Break Free' in the direction of sales and marketing.

Landing a job as a sales engineer with a multinational company at a campus placement felt like winning the lottery.

Watching my first boss charm customers with a smile and confidence sparked my interest in networking, meeting people, and—let's be real—made me more extroverted.

After a few years of sales experience and an MBA degree in the bag, a seemingly innocent job rotation landed me in the marketing communications function at Emerson Process Management. I thrived in this role, combining my technical know-how, sales skills and creativity. In 2001, I landed myself a communications role at L&T that taught me stakeholder management, B2B communications and how to thrive in a massive organisation. In 2004, I moved to the Tata Group (Tata Chemicals Limited) with the modest ambition of becoming the head of the communications function before I hit thirty. With legendary mentors and bosses like Prasad Menon, Homi Khusrokhan, R. Mukundan and B. Sudhakar guiding me, I flourished. Meeting and learning from icons like Ratan Tata and R. Gopalakrishnan were surreal, and I soaked up every bit of wisdom like a sponge in a rainstorm. My nine years there were a whirlwind of mentorship, leadership training, strategic thinking and international escapades. I even had the honour of leading the global rebranding of Tata Chemicals across four continents.

Along the way, I was lucky to pick up a few awards and the distinction of becoming one of India's first IABC-accredited business communicators. The journey was a constant cycle of raising the bar higher and higher, but each victory felt like a milestone I had worked my tail off to achieve.

By 2013, I hit a crossroads. Yes, it was one of those 'midlife crisis' moments where you question your entire existence. I felt the urge to make a more significant impact and to explore what I truly wanted to be known for. That's when I made the best impulsive decision of my life: I bought some farmland in Karjat. No wi-fi, no distractions, just me, the earth and a whole lot of questionable farming skills. But there is something deeply therapeutic about weekend farming—getting your hands dirty, planting vegetables and pretending you're a professional farmer. The returns on objectives (ROO) have been great!

Bagging the head of communications role at Godrej Group in 2013 was a dream come true. Shaping the company's reputation at a group level and sharing its story with over 1.1 billion consumers worldwide has been exciting. Working closely with the Godrej family, especially my boss Tanya Dubash, taught me the true meaning of humility, graciousness and meticulous attention to detail. Watching Adi Godrej, Nadir Godrej, Nisaba Godrej, Pirojsha Godrej and many stalwart CEOs and colleagues in action has reinforced the importance of valuing time, ethics in business, importance of diversity and nation building.

The last one decade at Godrej has been full of learnings, passionate brand building, reputation management, launching media properties, India's first in-house digital PR practice, a vertical for research-driven narratives and getting the freedom to experiment on multiple facets of holistic communications.

Well, our peers and the PR community have also recognised these efforts. At Godrej Industries Group, my team and I became the most awarded function in the country. I take immense pride in leading a team that has ranked number one six times in a row on the *Reputation Today* list of top communications teams in India.

During the lockdown, I co-authored a book, *The Pursuit of Reputation*. The book delves into the fascinating world of communications and branding. Hopefully, it has inspired some, demystified PR for some and helped some to reimagine the way they practise PR.

I derive a lot of joy from mentoring young professionals as it also enables me to be agile and updated. Sharing my knowledge and shaping the future of the profession through various professional body interventions and volunteering to teach at various B-schools is something I take immense pride in.

My mission has always been to create meaningful, lasting impressions across industries and communities. My professional journey has been a blend of serendipity, passion, curiosity, initiative, recognition and holistic growth, fueled by opportunities to connect with wonderful people and organisations, where I discovered my love for communications and got to shape some remarkable stories and global brand reputations. My achievements are a collective effort, and I am truly grateful to my fabulous team, mentors, consultancy partners, family, and the organisations I have worked for.

# 33

# Ramya Rajagopalan

## Lead - Marketing & Communications for Automation Business, Siemens

---

*'One thing that has remained constant is my belief that the buck stops with me.'*

I COME FROM A MIDDLE-CLASS FAMILY. I WAS BORN AND raised in Mumbai. . The focus on education was intense, and excelling in studies was a given. My father, now eighty-four, was ahead of his time—he completed an engineering degree and an MBA, which was quite rare in his era. He did his MBA from Fergusson College in Pune. My mother, an MSc in Zoology, was equally committed to academics. For both of them, academic rigour was non-negotiable.

I studied at Vani Vidyalaya in Mulund. For my graduation, I went to Somaiya, and later, pursued public relations and mass communication at XIC. During my college years, I briefly dabbled in the GNIIT programme at NIIT, trying my hand at C++ and coding. I completed it but quickly realised that sitting in front of a screen and coding all day was not for me.

Since pocket money was limited and I loved watching movies and going on outings with friends, I took up a summer internship with *The Indian Express* in Mumbai. I joined their Express Stars team as a trainee, selling advertising space. For them, it was a cost-effective way to hire talent, but for me, it was a gateway to a whole new world. *The Indian Express* was synonymous with courage and authentic journalism, and spending three months there exposed me to both the business and editorial sides of media. I learnt about sales, the financial mechanics of newspapers and how stories were identified, written and printed. I even stayed overnight at the office to witness the final stages of newspaper production. That experience consolidated my decision—I knew I wanted to work in communications, not tech.

At XIC, life came full circle when I landed an internship in corporate communications at Siemens. It was an exciting time for the company, and I got hands-on experience in internal communications, press releases and media outreach. Since Siemens did not have a PR consultancy at the time, I was deeply involved in groundwork—building press lists, coordinating announcements and learning the ropes of corporate communications. I was advised to start with a PR firm before moving into corporate communications.

Taking the advice of my mentors, I began applying to PR firms and landed a job at Clea Public Relations, one of the leading consultancies back then. It was an incredibly dynamic experience—I worked across entertainment, corporate, FMCG and tech sectors. But the most exciting project was launching BPL Mobile at a time when mobile phones were just entering the Indian market. The telecom boom was happening, and I was right in the middle of it. I spent about two-and-a-half to three years at Clea, working on some of the most exciting campaigns of that era. It was the perfect foundation for my career in communications.

I transitioned from Clea to Genesis in Mumbai. I spent a considerable amount of time working across the entertainment sector, spanning multiple businesses and geographies. After Mumbai, I moved to Genesis Bangalore, where I worked extensively in the tech space. However, one of the most memorable projects I handled was in the two-wheeler industry.

Back then, as a woman, riding a two-wheeler typically meant using a Kinetic, a non-gear scooter. But at Genesis, I had the opportunity to work with TVS at a pivotal time in their history. They had just ended their partnership with Suzuki and were establishing themselves as an independent brand, TVS Motor Company. I was part of the Genesis team supporting TVS in launching their first independent bike, the TVS Victor, across multiple regions. It was a fascinating experience, especially since they brought in Sachin Tendulkar as the brand ambassador.

Working at consultancies like Clea and Genesis helped me build a strong foundation. In a PR firm, you roll up your sleeves and do whatever it takes—there are no rigid roles or clear boundaries. If a major launch happened the night before, you were in the office by 6 a.m., tracking newspapers to provide media updates to clients.

After about five to six years in consultancies, I was fortunate to receive an opportunity to join Himalaya Pharma. At the time, Ravi Prasad was the CEO, and I was tasked with establishing their corporate communications department. Even today, Himalaya remains a privately held firm, despite being a multi-thousand-crore company.

Himalaya was a fantastic experience, but soon, an opportunity arose at Citibank. I moved on to lead communications for Citibank's Southern India market—my first role in an MNC. Transitioning from a privately held Indian company to a global financial institution was a completely different experience. The role exposed me to crisis management of a whole new level—handling bank frauds, collection issues and high-stakes crises.

I vividly recall an incident where a small van transporting cash to Citibank ATMs was hijacked, with approximately ₹1,900 crores stolen. It was front-page news, and our team had to manage the crisis, ensuring the right messaging, coordinating with law enforcement and handling media inquiries. While we were not directly involved in legal proceedings, we played a critical role in shaping Citibank's response and reputation management during such events.

Soon after, I moved to Britannia, which was a completely different experience. Like Himalaya, it was an Indian company but also a listed entity. This brought new responsibilities—investor relations, quarterly results and shareholder communications. The term QSQT (Quarter-Se-Quarter-Tak) defined the rhythm—every quarter, you had to justify performance and forecast the next three to six months. At the same time, Britannia was a fun FMCG brand, deeply connected to children and families. From launching new biscuit variants to exploring categories like cheese and milk, the work was dynamic and engaging.

After Britannia, I moved to Marico—again a listed FMCG company, but very different in its culture and operations. Marico was ahead of its time in areas we now widely discuss, such as employee empowerment, trust and autonomy, which were already embedded in its DNA fifteen to twenty years ago.

At this point, I decided to take a career break for about six to seven months. My son was around three-and-a-half, and I felt he was growing up too fast. At the time, six-month maternity leaves were not the norm. When he was just four months old, I had already resumed work at Himalaya, leaving him at daycare. While my career was always a priority, by the time I was at Marico, I felt the need to pause and spend more time with him.

I was not actively looking for a role when I reconnected with Prema Sagar. Beyond being a brilliant founder and thought leader, she had a unique way of staying in touch with former colleagues and employees. One day in Mumbai, we ran into each other, started chatting and she casually suggested that if I wanted to return to work, Genesis could be an option. So, I joined Genesis as a managing partner, overseeing the corporate vertical. My role involved bringing in business, mentoring teams and servicing clients.

The biggest shift from working in a corporate to a PR firm is how responsibility is structured. In a corporate, it is all on you, and maybe the CEO. As the head of communications, you own the company's reputation. But in a PR firm, you are the strategic partner, the hands and legs supporting corporate clients during crises, major announcements and day-to-day reputation management.

My time at Genesis was truly transformative, and I'll always be grateful to Prema for giving me the opportunity. It came at a particularly difficult phase in my life—I was going through a separation, but I never shared it with anyone, not even Prema. Yet, Genesis arrived at just the right moment, offering me exactly what I needed, both professionally and personally. The support I received, without ever having to voice my struggles, speaks volumes about the culture of the organisation.

Interestingly, life came full circle for me in an unexpected way. The HR head who had hired me at Britannia later moved to Siemens and reached out to me. He asked, 'Where are you working now?' When I told him I was a managing partner at Genesis, he responded, 'I'm looking for a head of communications at Siemens.'

When I spoke to Prema, she was candid: 'You thrive in fast-paced environments, managing multiple clients daily. Are you sure Siemens is right for you? It's a German company—it might be too slow, too structured. I'm worried you'll find it boring.' Looking back, I can say with certainty that there has never been a dull day at Siemens. Not then, not now, even after twelve years. Siemens, like Genesis and Marico, is an organisation that has its fundamentals right.

This culture of respect and meritocracy is something I have found in a few organisations—Marico, Genesis and Siemens. They set the standard for how companies should operate, valuing people for their capabilities rather than their personal circumstances.

My leadership style has evolved over time, shaped by my experiences and the people I have worked with. One thing that has remained constant is my belief that the buck stops with me. I empower my team to make decisions, and when they succeed, they get full credit. They are recognised, their names are put forward and they are given the visibility they deserve. But if something goes wrong, I take full responsibility. No one in my team takes the fall—that's on me.

Most of the time, people do not need you to solve their problems. They just need to know that you understand. A simple 'I see what you're going through' or 'I appreciate your efforts' can go a long way. If you can express that in an authentic and meaningful way, you have already won half the battle in building a strong and motivated team.

# 34

# Mukund Rajan

## FORMER BRAND CUSTODIAN, TATA SONS

―※―

*'Being inquisitive and keeping up with emerging trends will prevent stagnation and ensure growth.'*

I'M THE YOUNGEST OF FOUR CHILDREN. I WAS BORN IN Chennai, but for most of the years between my siblings' births and my own, and for a few years after, my family lived overseas. My father, an officer in the Indian Police Service, was assigned to Indian intelligence and worked in various embassies and high commissions as an intelligence officer.

From around 1964 to 1974, our family spent a decade in different capitals, starting with Jakarta in Indonesia, then Colombo in Sri Lanka and finally Brussels in Belgium. Though I was born in Chennai, my mother quickly returned to Jakarta with me to reunite with the rest of the family. These formative years gave us early exposure to diverse cultures and languages. While we experienced Asian cultures in Jakarta and Colombo, Brussels introduced us to European life. In fact, the first language I formally learnt in school was French, not English or Hindi.

Returning to India in 1974 was naturally a cultural adjustment. Settling in Delhi, my siblings and I had to adapt to Indian society and catch up on Hindi lessons with a tutor. However, having moved frequently, we quickly adapted to new environments and made friends easily. Those years undoubtedly nurtured my curiosity about global affairs and international relations.

Understanding my father's work as I grew older further fuelled my interest in international relations, eventually leading me to pursue it for my master's and doctorate after receiving a Rhodes Scholarship to Oxford. But before that, my academic journey in India followed a more conventional path.

In the 1970s and 1980s, career choices were limited. My older brothers pursued engineering through the IITs, setting an example that I followed. I too prepared for the Joint Entrance Examination, got selected and earned my engineering degree. Engineering was a practical choice given the stability and job prospects it offered. However, I never felt a strong passion for it.

My mother played a significant role in shaping us beyond academics. While she was a homemaker, she actively supported my father's responsibilities abroad, engaging in cultural and diplomatic functions. She was also a sports enthusiast who encouraged all of us to participate in various sports. We swam and played badminton, tennis and, once back in India, cricket.

This foundation in sports, combined with academics and leadership, helped me earn the Rhodes Scholarship. The scholarship values a combination of academic excellence, leadership abilities, extracurricular involvement and athletic pursuits. During my time at IIT Delhi, I served as the general secretary of the Student Affairs Council, captained the badminton team and maintained a solid academic performance. These experiences set me apart as one of the few IIT graduates to apply for and receive the Rhodes Scholarship.

What made my journey more unique was my decision to shift fields after receiving the scholarship. Leaving behind engineering, I pursued political science, a field aligned with my deepening interest in international relations. Looking back, I credit much of this direction to my father's career and the experiences I gained growing up in different parts of the world, observing global affairs first hand.

What particularly motivated me in the late 1980s, after finishing at IIT in 1989 and heading to Oxford from 1989 to 1994, was the significant impact Mikhail Gorbachev had on global politics.

Studying political science and international relations at such a pivotal time was enlightening. Although I had earned a degree in engineering, I found my true passion in understanding the broader context of global affairs. For my MPhil at Oxford, I needed to submit a 30,000-word dissertation. To connect my engineering background with my new academic interests, I explored an issue in environmental politics: the global debate over ozone depletion.

My research expanded into a doctoral dissertation, 'Global Environmental Politics: India and the North-South Politics of Global Environmental Issues'. I completed my doctorate between 1991 and 1994. The dissertation was later accepted for publication by Oxford University Press in 1995–96, becoming one of the first extensively researched works on Indian policy in global environmental issues.

Over the past decade and a half, my focus has shifted towards environmental, social and governance (ESG) issues.

This emphasis on sustainability has remained central to my career. Following my time at Oxford, I returned to India and interviewed with the Tata Administrative Service, further aligning my professional journey with my passion for environmental advocacy.

In 1994, the Tata Administrative Service (TAS) held a special round of interviews in September for candidates completing their degrees overseas. This was likely the last year they invited applications from international applicants, as their interviews usually took place earlier in the year.

I was particularly interested in exploring a corporate career with Tata for a couple of years. India had undergone significant changes during my time abroad. When I left in 1989, the country was still a protected socialist economy. By 1994, the economic reforms of 1991 had opened the market, attracting numerous multinationals. I wanted to understand how Indian companies were responding to this new competition.

Tata was the largest Indian conglomerate at the time, as it remains today. I wrote to them, and they invited me for an interview. The chairman of the interview panel was Ratan Tata himself. Following the interview, not only was I selected for a role within TAS, but Tata also left a message with the TAS secretary, indicating his wish for me to join his office after completing my first year of induction. This ultimately came to pass.

I initially planned to spend two years at Tata. My book, based on my doctoral dissertation, was about to be published, and I thought that if the corporate world did not suit me, I could transition to academia. However, I found myself thoroughly enjoying the experience, and what started as a two-year plan turned into a twenty-three-year career from 1995 to 2018.

Following my induction year, Ratan Tata invited me to join his office as an executive officer. I later became general manager, then vice president, essentially serving as his chief of staff for twelve years from 1996 to 2008. During the latter part of this period, I became deeply involved in Tata's telecom ventures, which were experiencing rapid growth and attracting significant capital investment. Tata appointed me to the boards of Tata Teleservices, Tata Teleservices Maharashtra and VSNL, later renamed Tata Communications.

In 2008, I transitioned to become the managing director of Tata Teleservices Maharashtra, a listed company holding licenses for Mumbai, Maharashtra and Goa. After two-and-a-half years in telecom, I moved to Tata Capital in 2010 to lead the Tata Opportunities Fund. This private equity fund was established to support unlisted Tata companies, particularly in the aftermath of the 2008 global financial crisis. The crisis had strained Tata's finances, particularly after the acquisitions of Jaguar Land Rover and Corus Steel. Traditional financing options became scarce, prompting the creation of the US $600 million Tata Opportunities Fund, which attracted significant global investment despite its inherently conflicted nature. During my time with the fund, we made successful investments in companies such as Tata Sky (now Tata Play), Tata Projects and Ginger Hotels.

My final move within the Tata Group was in 2012, at the request of newly appointed group chairman, the late Cyrus Mistry. He established a Group Executive Council (GEC) to shape Tata's leadership for the future, and I was one of five council members, two of whom were from within Tata. My role as brand custodian involved overseeing Tata's corporate brand management, ethics and sustainability efforts. I also served as chief ethics officer, administering the Tata Code of Conduct, and chaired the Sustainability Council to monitor Tata companies' corporate social responsibility (CSR) activities and their sustainability strategies.

In 2013, CSR became mandatory for companies of a specific size and scale criteria under the amendments to the Indian Companies Act. At that time, Tata's CSR spending amounted to around ₹600 crores annually, representing a significant contribution. My aim was to ensure alignment across the companies in their CSR activities.

As the brand custodian, I also oversaw Tata's corporate brand spending, served as the group spokesperson and managed Tata Sons' corporate communications, with oversight of the group companies' communication efforts. Additionally, I held board positions in some Tata companies and continued on the investment committee advisory board of the Tata Opportunities Fund, which I had helped establish. This phase was incredibly enriching, filled with learning and growth.

I worked closely with the late Cyrus Mistry for four years. However, 2016 saw a fallout between Cyrus and Ratan Tata, which has been widely discussed. It was a deeply saddening period, especially for those of us who were closely associated with both leaders. Having worked with Tata for twelve years and with Cyrus for four, I found the conflict unnecessary, driven by self-interest rather than the well-being of the Tata group.

After Cyrus' departure, Tata returned as interim chairman, eventually succeeded by N. Chandrasekaran. I remained with Tata for two more years, shifting roles to chair the sustainability council and continue as the chief ethics officer. However, I stepped down from my corporate communications and brand custodian responsibilities and took on the oversight of Tata Sons' global offices.

In 2018, after feeling that I had contributed all I could at Tata, I decided to pursue entrepreneurship. My wife, a successful entrepreneur, had inspired me. Having worked for a major bank, she established her own company in 2011, a multi-family office that has become India's largest independent wealth management firm for high-net-worth individuals. Observing her success over the years gave me the confidence to venture out on my own.

Turning fifty in 2018 also marked a point of reflection and a desire to try something different. Along with some former Tata colleagues, I founded ECube, a firm centred around ESG (Environmental, Social and Governance) solutions. ECube's goal is to help Indian businesses understand the importance of ESG and provide relevant solutions. Our primary focus is on mid-market companies, leveraging both our Tata experience and recent insights.

During the COVID-19 pandemic, I authored a book, *Outlast: How ESG Can Benefit Your Business*. Prior to that, I wrote *Brand Custodian: My Years in the Tatas*, capturing my experiences and reflections on my time at the company.

More recently, I co-authored *Tata's Leadership Experiment: The Story of the Tata Administrative Service* with Sonu Bhasin and Bharat Wakhlu. This project stemmed from the desire of TAS alumni to document the legacy and history of the service, especially as some of its early members had passed away. Looking back, it's been a fulfilling thirty-year journey, with Tata at the heart of it all.

A significant learning is the importance of continuous learning. With the rapid pace of technological advancements, like the current rise of generative AI, staying curious and informed is essential. For communications professionals, understanding technological innovations and leveraging them effectively is no longer optional. Being inquisitive and keeping up with emerging trends will prevent stagnation and ensure growth.

Even now, well past fifty, I dedicate time to learning about areas like technology, climate change and sustainability. This mindset has allowed me to stay relevant and effective in my career.

I have also been fortunate to have had mentors like Ratan Tata and Cyrus Mistry, who offered me autonomy and responsibility at a young age. Their trust motivated me to meet high expectations and excel. If you find leaders who empower you, work diligently to earn their confidence. Their mentorship can shape your career and open doors to new opportunities.

It's also essential not to put leaders or role models on pedestals. While admiration is natural, it's important to remember that every successful person has flaws, failures and setbacks. Understanding that no one is infallible helps maintain perspective and resilience when faced with challenges. Conversely, never underestimate your own potential. Each of us has the ability to achieve greatness through smart work, perseverance and a bit of luck.

During my time as a managing director in telecom, I often told my colleagues that anyone, whether in finance, HR or operations, could become a CEO with the right mindset and determination. Leadership is not confined to titles. In personal lives too, parents, caregivers and community leaders are already demonstrating leadership. The scale may differ but the core qualities of responsibility, vision and care remain the same.

Ultimately, the grass may appear greener on the other side, but every opportunity comes with its own set of challenges. Recognising your own capabilities and embracing continuous growth will allow you to thrive, regardless of the circumstances.

# 35

# Senjam Raj Sekhar

## HEAD - GLOBAL COMMUNICATIONS, MPL

---

*'I'm deeply thankful for the journey—every twist, turn and early morning run included.'*

While I was born in Shillong, my earliest memories take me back to the sleepy town of Along in Arunachal Pradesh, perched close to the Chinese border. That's where I spent most of my early childhood, immersed in nature. Our family eventually made Guwahati home, where I finished my schooling—first at Don Bosco up to Class 10, then at Cotton College for Classes 11 and 12. Guwahati shaped much of my teenage years, but by the time school was done, I was ready for something bigger. Delhi beckoned. I packed my bags and made the leap to the capital, where I dived into English Literature at Ramjas College. Later, I followed that up with a degree in law from the Campus Law Centre at Delhi University. After finishing my law exams, I decided to stay back in Delhi during the summer break. With legal internships drying up during court vacation time, I stumbled into PR. This was 1995.

Consultancies like Perfect Relations and IPAN were just making their mark. I applied to Perfect Relations, cracked a current affairs test and landed my first job. What started as a stopgap turned into a career. Back then, most people drifted into PR from other fields—I was a rare case of diving into it straight out of college.

Quizzing played a big role in my life and my chosen profession of PR. Quizzing is not just about knowing random facts—it's about connecting the dots. In 1997, I began writing a weekly quiz column for *The Asian Age*. It started as a Sunday feature, and it's still going strong. Now in its twenty-eighth year, it holds the record as the longest-running quiz column in a mainstream Indian newspaper.

From Perfect Relations, I moved through consultancies like Good Relations, Weber Shandwick and Genesis. Each had its moments, but a few experiences stand out.

Like the time I was handling PR for McDonald's when they admitted in a US court case that their fries contain beef flavouring. Massive protests broke out in India. The MD was about to leave for a family vacation. He appointed me the official spokesperson for McDonald's India. For the next two weeks, I was taking every call, giving every quote, managing a storm.

The second came courtesy of BPCL. It all started with a routine stop at a petrol station in Chanakyapuri. As I waited for my tank to fill, something caught my eye—something almost unheard of in 1999. The person dispensing fuel was a woman. Intrigued, I struck up a conversation and found that a few women had recently started working at the pump. It was unusual, refreshing—and instantly, an idea sparked. The next day, I called my client at BPCL with a bold pitch: what if we turned this into India's first all-women-run petrol station? It was a company-owned, company-operated (COCO) outlet, which meant we had the flexibility to make that vision real.

To BPCL's credit, they did not hesitate. The male staff were reassigned, a female manager was appointed and even the security guards were women. It was not just a gesture—it was a statement.

Two months later, on 8 March, International Women's Day, we threw open the gates to India's first all-women petrol pump. The media loved it. The news landed on the front pages of nearly every major newspaper in the country. Even now, years later, that petrol pump is still run entirely by women.

My journey in corporate communications kicked off at Samsung, but the turning point was when I joined the Bharti Group. I spent nearly seven years there, during one of the most exciting periods in India's telecom history. The industry was booming, and I was part of the fascinating journey to connect a billion Indians and make communication accessible to everyone. Then came Vedanta. We also took Vedanta digital—building a real social media presence in an industry where transparency was rare. And it worked.

It was at Vedanta that I took the boldest decision of my life. I had always dreamt of hitting pause and exploring the world, and I took the plunge in 2013. This was not just holiday hopping but deep travel. We covered fifteen countries, spending around a month in each country—from South America to Europe and Asia. We immersed ourselves in the local rhythms, eating where the locals ate, learning the stories and navigating life as they lived it.

Out of nowhere, Flipkart came calling. I was fielding interviews over patchy Skype calls. Before I knew it, I was trading backpacks for a start-up life. For now, I have done fifty-eight countries and still counting.

When I joined Flipkart, the company was already a household name. But with scale came scrutiny. Every customer complaint, every leadership change, every misstep—real or perceived—was amplified. We needed more than press releases and media outreach. We needed to own our story.

That's how Flipkart Stories was born—not as a typical corporate blog, but as a bold experiment in humanising e-commerce. We did not want to just talk about delivery speeds or deals. We wanted to show how Flipkart was quietly reshaping India—one customer, one town, one package at a time.

Now at MPL, some of the most meaningful work I do is centred around Gaming for Good—using the power of play to drive real-world impact and positive change.

The first was 'Missing', a game developed to raise awareness about human trafficking. But this was not just a game—it was a lifeline. Designed to educate players on the warning signs of trafficking, 'Missing' was launched in ten languages to reach communities most at risk. By combining gameplay with education, we created an experience that did not just engage, but empowered.

The second initiative was 'Gamers for Dementia', a nationwide campaign to bring attention to one of India's growing health concerns. With India home to the second-highest number of dementia cases globally, we focused on the role gaming can play in delaying cognitive decline, particularly among homebound seniors. We rallied over half a million gamers to spend quality time with elderly family members, encouraging intergenerational bonding through games that stimulate mental activity. It was not just about awareness, it was about connection, compassion and using play to improve lives.

Having spent nearly thirty years in communications—since 1995—I have seen the field transform in ways I never imagined. And looking back, I am deeply thankful for the journey—every twist, turn and early morning run included.

# 36

# Pragnya Ram

GROUP EXECUTIVE PRESIDENT & GROUP HEAD
CSR - LEGACY DOCUMENTATION & ARCHIVES,
ADITYA BIRLA GROUP

*'Success is beyond perseverance or competence, it's about context, confidence, compassion and above all character. Being mindful, humble and always on the learning curve is equally important.'*

BORN AND RAISED IN MUMBAI, I HAVE BEEN A GLOBETROTTER, given my career trajectory. My academic journey has been one of dedication and excellence. After earning a master's in history and sociology, I pursued a post-graduate degree in journalism, followed by a PhD from Bombay University. Throughout my studies, I was a topper.

I began my career in academics, teaching in some of the best colleges in the country, such as Elphinstone and St Xavier's in Mumbai and then Stella Maris in Chennai, when Ram, my husband, moved out of Mumbai.

When we returned to Mumbai, I faced a situation: there were no teaching vacancies in the middle of the term. Since I had studied journalism, the Bombay Management Association invited me to lead their communications department. As the editor of their management journal, I had the opportunity to interview managing directors of large reputed companies.

Again, I have been singularly fortunate in working with very good organisations. First Crompton Greaves for a decade, followed by Ciba Geigy for more than a decade and now at Aditya Birla Group for nearly three decades.

Kumar Mangalam Birla, our group chairman, and Rajashreeji Birla, chairperson, Aditya Birla Centre for Community Initiatives and Rural Development, are my role models. I joined the Aditya Birla Group in 1997. This was a turning point in my life. When I met Kumar Mangalam Birla in 1996, he was in his late twenties and I in my late forties. I have been incredibly fortunate to have been named by our chairman to be an important part of this transformative journey, as group head of communications and CSR.

My affinity and close connection to the brand gives me an innate sense of pride and happiness. I know I belong. In my heart I know that collectively through our CSR and group our endeavour is to make the world a better place, a force for good. Let me dwell a bit on our Aditya Birla Scholarships Programme, which pays homage to our visionary and iconic founder Aditya Vikram Birla and second, our core vision is to spawn tomorrow's leaders today.

Our overarching goal is to make it to the top, the best scholarship so to say. We tied up with institutes of excellence such as IITs and IIMs to begin with. When we look back, from where we began and where we have reached, the track record is indeed fulfilling. We have supported 350 amazing individuals, entrepreneurs, unicorns, founders, bureaucrats, professionals in the consulting firms, academics and scientists. In all humility, it does seem like we have pulled off a miracle.

I am indeed blessed to continue long after the age of superannuation and head a portfolio carved out for me. Since 2021, I have been able to set up the Aditya Birla Centre for Archival Research and have a professional team of archivists engaged in the venture. Likewise, a team of journalists who have set up a communications company are involved in capturing the outstanding legacy of our group's companies— Grasim and Hindalco to begin with.

One of the most gratifying CSR projects has been our involvement in public health, such as our efforts to combat polio. We have administered over a million doses, and Amitabh Bachchan recently highlighted this work on *Kaun Banega Crorepati*, emphasising how we have helped put India on the global map.

At the end of the day some of the lessons that I have learnt on the road to life:

a. Believe everything will work out and it will.
b. You have to come to terms with your life.
c. Success and suffering are both generic. No one is unscathed. Likewise, success never goes unnoticed.
d. Believe in the divine.
e. God, your family, your boss and your workplace keep you glued to life.

And last of all, there is much more to be said, that is left unsaid.

# 37

# Debasis Ray

## FORMER HEAD - CORPORATE COMMUNICATIONS, TATA TRUSTS

*'I hold myself to the highest standards, leading by example and guiding team members to master these standards.'*

I WAS BORN IN KOLKATA. MY FATHER WAS IN THE INDIAN Railways and my mother was a homemaker. I have always been a communicator—first as a journalist for five years and then in the corporate world for over thirty-two years. I joined *The Telegraph* straight out of college, shortly after its launch in 1982. At that time, we were up against *The Statesman*, one of India's top English newspapers. Our objective was simple: to overtake them.

Under the mentorship of industry stalwarts, I honed two vital skills: identifying news hidden within data and information, and presenting it in a compelling way. These skills have been invaluable in my career, both as an operating manager and as a leader. In March 1991, I joined Hindustan

Unilever's (HUL) communications team, led by the legendary Irfan Khan. At that time, HUL was already a giant, and with Unilever merging its subsidiaries, the company was becoming even larger. I had the privilege of working in Kolkata, Mumbai, Bangalore and London, providing communications support across brands, mergers, acquisitions, corporate strategy and crises.

I recall three pivotal engagements. First in August 1997. The regulator made a false insider trading allegation against HUL. The news was leaked selectively, and the board, including Khan, were in Bangalore. I had to manage the crisis, briefing the chairman and handling media calls until we disproved the allegation in September 1998. Then in 1997, Pepsodent launched a new formulation with the claim of being '102 per cent better' than competitors, sparking a media battle. I worked closely with the brand team to shape our media campaign and achieve significant visibility. Last in 1999, I was seconded to Unilever's corporate communications team in London, working on scripting the chairman's speech to announce a major strategic shift at their annual review with global leadership.

Irfan Khan taught me an invaluable lesson. Every corporate action exists within a broader context, shaped by both internal dynamics and the ever-changing external environment. A communicator's role is to understand and convey this context, ensuring that the organisation is attuned to it.

From July 2005 to June 2023, I worked in various Tata companies and Tata Trusts, initially as head of corporate communications at Tata Motors, and later as chief of group corporate communications and spokesperson at Tata Sons, as well as head of corporate communications at Tata Trusts. When I joined Tata Motors, the company was no longer among

India's most respected companies, though it retained some of its equity. My goal was to restore its reputation. By 2007, after expanding both the domestic and international businesses, Tata Motors was rated among the top ten in several surveys.

The unveiling of the Nano and the acquisition of Jaguar Land Rover (JLR) in 2008 helped bolster the company's narrative. Leading communications for the Nano from its inception, through its launch and associated crises, to its commercial success was a significant achievement. Likewise, managing the narrative around the JLR acquisition required effective communication to convince the media about Tata Motors' ability to manage successful international operations.

In my role at Tata Sons, I was tasked with strengthening media and social media functions. A key accomplishment was bringing together the group companies to present a unified narrative. Without executive control, this was achieved through persuasion, demonstrating how such a narrative could highlight the strengths of each company.

One of the most intense moments of my career came when Tata Sons replaced the late Cyrus Mistry as chairman. Communicating the rationale behind this decision was crucial, and it further strengthened Tata's reputation as India's most respected institution.

This shift at Tata Sons brought the role of Tata Trusts into focus. The Trusts, previously a silent actor, needed to communicate their work more consistently. We initiated a campaign to ensure that their contributions to national issues were recognised. Over time, the Trusts have grown to be a reference point in their fields.

I have always built teams based on complementarity, seeking individuals who are stronger than I am in areas where I am weak. I hold myself to the highest standards, leading by example and guiding team members to master these standards. Once I am confident in the team's ability, they are empowered to act on decisions that we have all agreed upon. When actions succeed, they are front and centre; when they fail, I take responsibility and stand behind them. My greatest satisfaction after two decades of nurturing and leading talented individuals is seeing many of them rise to leadership positions in companies across various industries.

# 38

# Minari Shah

### FORMER DIRECTOR - COMMUNICATIONS, AMAZON INDIA

---

*'I firmly believe that our role as communicators is to hold up a mirror to the business, offering honest feedback and perspective.'*

I SPENT MOST OF MY EARLY LIFE IN A SMALL TOWN CALLED Bhilai in Madhya Pradesh until I was fifteen. My dad, an engineer, worked with SAIL, the steel plant there. A few years later, we moved to Vizag, when my dad started working at RINL, another steel plant, and I completed the last three years of my schooling there.

College life in Chennai was incredible. I went to Stella Maris, and while I was initially quiet and reserved, I slowly became more confident and started enjoying my time there. My first year was filled with long letters to my parents, documenting all the new experiences and the excitement of learning new things.

After college, I decided to apply to JNU. It was not planned at all, but I loved history and was naturally inclined toward it. I did not prepare much for the entrance exam but managed to get in, which confirmed for me that following what I loved made more sense than following a prescribed path. During my time at JNU, I also prepared for the UPSC exams. At first, I thought becoming a bureaucrat was the right choice, but after clearing the first two rounds, I paused and really questioned whether that was what I wanted. I decided not to attend the interview, a decision that I have never regretted. It felt like the right thing to do for me. I was at a crossroads, unsure about what to do next, compounded by some personal upheavals and tragedies during that time. I had moved back to Chennai, where my parents were living, and was trying to figure out my next step.

One day, a young cousin of mine asked if I could accompany her to Loyola College as she needed to check out some courses. I agreed, and when we arrived, the college was closed, so she could not gather any information. But there was a half-torn sticker on a bulletin board advertising a job opening, with a phone number. It was a simple message, but it caught my attention. I walked over to a public phone booth and called the number. The person I needed to speak with was not available that morning, but I was asked to call back later. When I did, they offered me an interview. I went in, and they asked me to take a copywriting test. At that time, I had no idea what a copy test was, and I'd never considered a career in advertising or anything related. But I decided to give it a try and found the experience really enjoyable. A couple of days later, they called back and offered me the job. And that became my first professional role, though not technically my first job.

So, my first real job, in a sense, was in Chennai, where I worked as a copywriter for about three years. After that, I realised I had outgrown the role and was ready for something new. I had always wanted to move to Mumbai and felt it was time for a change. I had a couple of copywriting offers from large agencies like Ogilvy, but they were only offering positions in Chennai or Bangalore, not Mumbai.

Around that time, I saw an ad in *The Hindu Business Line* for a features analyst position. The job was available in Chennai, Delhi or Mumbai and, although I did not know anything about journalism, I knew I wanted to work in Mumbai, so I applied. I interviewed, got the job and moved to Mumbai. I worked as a journalist at *Business Line* and *Business India*, and during this time, I got married to someone I had met at work. We were both journalists and became close friends before eventually marrying. I joined Sampark, where Rajan and Bela were incredibly kind and supportive. I was very open with them about needing a job for financial reasons, and they understood. I worked with them for just six months but I have a lot of respect for Rajan, as he was one of the first PR professionals I truly admired.

I moved to Mahindra thereafter. After a year with Mahindra, I found myself at another crossroads. Personally, things had taken a positive turn—we were no longer drowning in debts and loans for the first time in our lives. One random day, I turned to my husband and said, 'You know, if there's one thing I wish I had done earlier in life, it's filmmaking. I absolutely love cinema, and I wish I had pursued filmmaking when I was younger.' He looked at me and simply said, 'So do it.' I was taken aback. I started to explore the idea. A colleague from *Business India* connected me with an editor from a well-known filmmaker's team, and that led to more connections.

Within months, I found myself with an opportunity to join a film production as an assistant director. I shared my aspirations with my boss, Anand Mahindra. He was incredibly supportive and said, 'If this is something you really want to try, go ahead.'

I spent about three years working in the film industry. However, only one film I worked on ever made it to theatres. A lot of projects were developed, but for various reasons, they never came to fruition. The one film I worked on extensively, which I was originally brought in for scripting and as an assistant director, was delayed repeatedly. The lead actor, Shah Rukh Khan, had to undergo back surgery, which delayed the production. The film was *Chalte Chalte*, which was his production. Due to his surgery, the shoot and everything around it was postponed, and it took much longer to get the film off the ground. The experience in the film industry was rewarding but it was also financially unsustainable. So, I made the decision to return to PR.

I joined L&T Infotech. I really enjoyed my time there. I never imagined, though, that one day I would launch Prime Video in India. At the time, the industry and my film experience seemed unrelated to anything corporate. But years later, when Prime Video launched in India, my background in cinema suddenly became relevant. That's the thing I always tell people: you never know how your experiences will connect later on.

After about ten or eleven months, I got a call from NCR, the company that handles ATMs and retail technologies. It was my first job with an international company, an American firm. By the end of four years, I started feeling saturated and was not sure about what to do next. I decided to resign. A former contact told me that Dell had a potential opening in Bangalore, and though I did not initially have all the details, I said yes to exploring it. After five years at Dell, I received an offer from HSBC. At the time, I was not sure how far I could progress in a tech company while living outside Mumbai, so I decided it was a good opportunity to explore a financial company.

However, as time went on, I realised that the banking industry was not quite for me. Nothing against the industry, but I found that I was more passionate about tech. So, I decided to stay a bit longer, but I knew I wanted my next step to be with an Indian company. The Tata Group seemed like a natural fit.

A month later, I got a call from Tata Motors. Initially, I was not sure since I had only been with HSBC for about nine months. But after meeting the HR head, Prabir Jha, and eventually the MD, I realised this was an opportunity I could not pass up. I stayed with Tata Motors for four years, and then I got a call from Amazon. Initially, I hesitated because I was not keen on leaving Mumbai, but after several discussions, I decided to explore the opportunity. The Amazon job has been the longest tenure of my career. I started as the India PR lead with a team of just eight people, managing everything from devices to retail, logistics and Prime Video launches.

The most significant aspect of my journey had been expanding our team into new areas. One of the biggest milestones was launching Amazon India's 'Own Channel Strategy', which included the Amazon India Newsroom, our social media handles and the About Amazon platform. It was incredible to lead the creation and execution of communications strategies for different Amazon businesses. The scale, complexity and diversity of this experience across multiple markets will always be etched in my memory.

When people are new to working with me, they might initially find me a bit abrasive or demanding. However, over time, I believe they come to understand that I genuinely care about the people I work with and that I value fresh ideas. Fairness and justice are deeply important to me, and I always strive to embody those values in my leadership.

# 39

# Amandeep Singh

## SVP - Marketing & Communications, Indraprastha Gas Limited

---

*'Keep planting small seedlings as you move along the journey of life by nurturing relationships and staying transparent.'*

I HAIL FROM JALANDHAR IN PUNJAB, THOUGH MY FAMILY WAS traditionally rooted in Amritsar. I spent the initial years of my childhood playing on the streets of Amritsar and then we moved to Chandigarh.

Growing up in the 1970s, as part of what is now called Generation X, I saw first-hand the aspirations of our parents. They belonged to a generation that had spent their childhood in the aftermath of India's independence, with many in the border states having endured the trauma of Partition. Having lived through such upheaval, they placed immense value on education, seeing it as the key to securing a better future for their children. Their hopes and investments in education were driven by the belief that as India evolved, the next generation would rise to lead and shape the nation's progress.

After completing my secondary education, I initially pursued life sciences with the hope of becoming a doctor. However, that path did not work out. Instead, I found myself drawn to communication and writing—subjects I naturally excelled in. In the pre-internet era, newspapers were highly revered, and anything printed in them was considered the absolute truth. While growing up, I was always fascinated by various media platforms and even listened attentively to radio stations from across the world during my teenage days.

After graduating, I pursued an MBA in the early 1990s, when business education was gaining popularity. I was fortunate to secure admission locally in Punjab and completed my degree. My first job was with the Indian Express Group in Chandigarh, where I worked in space marketing. While I had a deep interest in media and publications, I initially did not fully grasp the difference between marketing and other communication roles.

Over time, my fascination with media led me to explore journalism further. I pursued a part-time diploma in journalism, hoping to carve a path in communications. My experience in space marketing in newspapers led me to space marketing for exhibitions, when I switched to the Confederation of Indian Industry (CII) in Chandigarh.

In 1998, I got the opportunity to join the India Trade Promotion Organisation (ITPO) in Delhi, the body responsible for managing the Pragati Maidan Complex. By then, I had experience in media, a diploma in journalism and a growing understanding of the communication business. ITPO considered me for a role in the Public Relations department, given my background in media and communication. They were not aware that I had been working in marketing, but when they asked if I'd be willing to try PR, I decided to give it a shot. Fortunately, I quickly developed a liking for the field.

That marked my transition from hardcore sales and marketing to a communications-focused role in PR after five years of work experience. At ITPO, we managed India's largest exhibition, the India International Trade Fair, along with several other major trade fairs. I was fortunate to have incredible mentors who taught me the nuances of the business. Even today, whenever I write a press release or work with advertising agencies, I follow the models they had introduced me to. I remain grateful to Somnath Sarkar and Soma Chakravarty, whom I still consider my mentors in the field of communication.

ITPO also provided me with a remarkable opportunity to expand my horizons internationally. They sent me to Germany for a year-long advanced training programme in trade fair management. This marked another significant transition in my career—from a national platform to an international one. It was around the turn of the century in 2001–02, when India was on the brink of rapid economic expansion.

By the time I returned from Germany, I realised that a traditional public sector job was not aligned with what I truly wanted for my career. Then, as luck would have it, I received a call from a job placement consultant about an opportunity to head communications for an emerging city gas distribution company.

The organisation was Indraprastha Gas Limited (IGL), which had already begun expanding Delhi's CNG network in 2005 to fuel a large number of vehicles. At the time, the transition to CNG was a hot topic, with frequent media coverage about long queues at fuelling stations and public concerns over infrastructure challenges. Managing media relations in such a high-stakes environment was not easy.

However, being in my mid-thirties, with some experience under my belt, I was at the perfect stage to take on new challenges and prove myself. Looking back, joining IGL in 2005 was one of the most pivotal decisions of my life—one that shaped the next two decades of my professional journey.

Today, with over thirty years of experience, I can proudly say that twenty of those years have been with this organisation. My journey here has been deeply intertwined with the organisation's own growth, and I cannot overlook the impact it has had on me. The company and I grew together.

When I joined, the company had a turnover of just ₹500 crores, with profits around ₹100 crores. Today, we are closing in on ₹20,000 crores in revenue, with profits soaring to around ₹1,500 crores. The transformation has been incredible.

In the early days, we were a small, close-knit team operating solely in Delhi. My role was focused on corporate communications, primarily media relations. This was just before the rise of social media, a time when traditional media held immense influence—news coverage could make or break reputations. Back then, we had an entire day to respond to media queries. With the advent of television news, that window shrank to a few hours. Today, with social media, we do not even have a few minutes.

Operating a public utility company in the national capital comes with its own set of challenges. Being in the energy sector meant we were always under intense scrutiny, and any issue—no matter how small—could turn into a major story. However, despite facing occasional crises, we have successfully navigated them with transparency and effective communication.

Managing communications for a listed public utility means balancing two distinct media audiences. On one end, there's the national business media, focused on top-line growth, bottom-line margins, EBITDA and investor returns. On the other, there's the city and consumer-focused media, catering to everyday users and the general public, who perceive price hikes as a burden. While shareholders may see price adjustments as a positive for margins, the common man often views them as profiteering.

Ultimately, my role has been about relationship-building, and being based in Delhi—where national media operates—has been a tremendous advantage. The trust and rapport I have built over the years have been instrumental in shaping the organisation's communication strategy and reputation.

As the primary fuel provider for Delhi's public transport system—autos, taxis and buses—we had a direct connection with the city's driver community, which was largely unorganised. After the Nirbhaya incident, concerns around public transport safety intensified, and as a key stakeholder, we recognised our responsibility to engage with this community.

This led to one of our most impactful CSR initiatives—a gender sensitisation programme for public transport drivers. The campaign ran from 2015 to 2022, and if you have travelled in Delhi, you might have noticed stickers on autos and taxis saying 'This taxi respects women' or *'Mera imaan, mahilaon ka samman'* (I believe in respect for women). Initially launched with the Delhi government, the campaign later expanded to Gurgaon and Noida as well. The programme linked gender sensitisation training to the renewal of fitness certificates for auto and taxi drivers, thus making it mandatory.

Another major initiative, Move Without Fear, focused on self-defence training for adolescent girls in government schools, empowering them to travel independently. The impact assessment of Move Without Fear revealed a powerful insight—when a girl learns her first self-defence move, she sheds inhibitions and gains the confidence to navigate the world fearlessly. This boost in confidence fuels aspirations, encouraging them to pursue education and careers despite societal constraints.

Around 2022, I transitioned into a core marketing role, taking on the responsibility of heading the marketing for the piped natural gas business. My role involves managing a customer base of nearly three million, overseeing CRM, billing, receivables, new connections, seamless supply and complaint management. Additionally, I handle the industrial and commercial segment, catering to around 12,000 businesses and driving growth in that space.

For the first year, I stepped away from communication, focusing solely on marketing. However, a year later, I found myself back in the communication role as well. Communication has always been my first love. While I continue to lead the marketing of the piped gas segment, I also manage corporate communications, given my long-standing relationships and deep understanding of the organisation's brand narrative.

Reflecting on my journey, I often recall the wisdom of one of my strategic management professors—he emphasised planting small seedlings as we move along the way in the journey of our life, nurturing relationships and staying transparent and honest. These principles have guided my career, reinforcing the importance of long-term trust and credibility in communication.

# 40

# Atul Takle

FORMER EVP - CORPORATE COMMUNICATIONS,
SKS MICROFINANCE

---

*'I do not believe in "gardening leave". If you stop moving, your mind slows down. That's not me. I plan to keep contributing, learning and staying sharp.'*

I WAS BORN IN PUNE. INTERESTINGLY, I DO NOT HAVE A BIRTH certificate. Pune was hit by devastating floods at the time, caused by its two rivers overflowing. I was born in a hospital located on the banks of one of the rivers that was badly affected, and in the chaos, my birth records were lost. So, to this day, the only official proof of my birthdate is my school leaving certificate.

My father, who was an alumnus of the Scindia School, thought it might be a good place for me too. I was about seven or eight when I sat for the entrance exam and got selected. And just like that, we packed up and went off to Gwalior from Kolkata, where my father was posted.

My proudest moment was becoming the youngest house captain in Class 11 (I was already the youngest school prefect in Class 10)—and leading my house to win the Best House Award. It was extra special because the school's honours board listed my name: Atul Takle, House Captain, 1972. The last name from our house on that board was from 1942—my father. For thirty years, our house had won nothing that matched this achievement.

During my Class 10 and 11, my father was transferred from Kolkata to Mumbai, so I returned to Mumbai after completing my studies. After finishing my ISC exams in December, I had a six-month gap before college began in June. To pass the time, I started learning German at the Max Müller Bhavan.

Later, I joined Sydenham College to study economics. While most of my peers pursued CA or MBA, I chose to continue with German. I completed advanced courses, studied further in Pune and even received a scholarship to study in Heidelberg, Germany, where I got a job as a German-English interpreter in East Germany, near Berlin. I worked there for a year and a half.

When I returned home, my father asked me what I wanted to do. He said, 'If you want to study, I'll support you. But if you want to work, you're on your own.' I told him I'd figure it out. Then a school friend at Philips told me about an opening for sales officers. I applied, and after a group discussion, I was called in by Steven Pinto, the sales director. He asked, 'How do you feel about going to Saharanpur?' I replied, 'I'm not going to Saharanpur.' He said that's where they sent all trainees. I declined the job. He looked at me and said, 'You're a confused young man, aren't you?' 'Maybe,' I admitted.

He then asked what I thought about advertising. I told him I knew nothing about it. He then said, 'I'll send you to someone who might help,' and connected me with his brother, Stanley Pinto, a director at Lintas.

I took a cab to Nariman Point and met Stanley. I told him upfront I knew little about advertising. He asked if I remembered any campaigns, and I mentioned the Mapro peas ad, 'peas, peas, peas'. That struck a chord, and he introduced me to two of his assistants, Ajay Shrikhande and Chintamani Rao. They spent an hour grilling me on basic questions—testing my common sense—and then asked me to wait. I was hired. Advertising turned out to be the right fit. That's where I discovered my eye for detail—my real strength. Even if something did not have a comma where it should, I would catch it.

Around this time, I got married. My wife worked in operations at the Taj, and I was putting in long hours in advertising. Our schedules left us little time together, so we moved to Pune and lived with my grandparents for three years. That's where our son, Abhishek, was born. That is when I dabbled in political advertising for the BJP's Marathi campaign, which created connections that helped me later.

When our son developed infantile asthma, the doctor recommended a humid climate. So, we moved back to Mumbai. I joined *The Indian Express* as a consultant, building an in-house ad agency for the group. After five years, I decided to leave. Around then, Manu Chhabria offered me a role at Jumbo Electronics in Dubai. It was short-lived—about a year and a half—but impactful. Though I was not hired for PR, I found myself handling it when his company Shaw Wallace in India faced media scrutiny. That was my real initiation into the world of PR.

One key moment came when a misleading postscript was added to a rebuttal I'd drafted. I had not written it, but it was sent under my name. That breach of trust was my cue to leave. Chhabria tried to persuade me to stay, but I had made up my mind. My wife and son flew back to India, and I wrapped up in Dubai before returning—jobless.

I tapped into my network and learnt of an opening at RPG. Though they had already made an offer to someone else, I met with their HR leadership. When asked about my past with Chhabria, I responded frankly, 'You haven't offered me the job yet—and your group had a JV with him. You probably know him better than I do.' That honesty must have worked. A few days later, they called and I got the job.

Joining RPG was a turning point. It was a large, diversified group, and I was like a sponge—absorbing everything. I got to learn about tyres (CEAT), tea (Harrisons Malayalam), retail (Foodworld), power generation, transmission (CESC) and even hospitality (RPG owned Taj Connemara). It was an incredible journey in the late 1990s.

Out of the blue, Romit Chatterjee (a senior leader at Tata Sons) called and asked, 'Would you like to join the Tatas?' He had two roles—one at Indian Hotels, the other at TCS. I chose TCS. A meeting with S. Ramadorai was arranged. The interview was brief—Ramadorai was rushing to the US. He asked, 'What do you guys actually do?' Then paused and said, 'Don't answer. Just send me a three-slide deck on how communications can help TCS—before I land.' I did. Two days later I was hired.

Around then, during the TCS IPO roadshow, I got a call from Accenture with a job offer. I joined Accenture. Meanwhile, my personal life was stretched—my wife and son were in Mumbai, parents in Pune, and I was in Bangalore. While en route to Atlanta to collect a coveted award, I stopped over in Dubai for a couple of days with a friend. That's when my sister messaged: 'Pa is no more.' I flew back for the funeral and knew things had to change. I could no longer stay alone in Bangalore, leave my mother alone in Pune with my wife and son in Mumbai, so I decided to leave Accenture.

Around then, Sanjay Jog (then at Future Group) reached out, asking if I was moving back to Mumbai. He took me to meet Kishore Biyani. Kishoreji did not make eye contact but asked what I thought of the challenge. I said, 'If you're David facing Goliath, read *The Art of War*.' Apparently, that was enough, and I got the job.

A few years later, Anjali Bansal from Spencer Stuart invited me for coffee and asked if I was ready to take a 'leap of faith'. That leap turned out to be SKS Microfinance. I knew nothing about microfinance, but after meeting Vikram Akula in Hyderabad, I was intrigued—especially by the idea of working in villages and wearing a kurta-pyjama to office. After this stint I eventually moved back to Mumbai, continuing as a consultant to help rebrand SKS. The company was finally acquired by a bank and came to be called Bharat Financial Inclusion.

In Mumbai, I reconnected with Rajesh Chaturvedi and joined Adfactors PR, initially managing communications for Vodafone. Over time, I led high-impact mandates for Infosys, Cisco and L&T. I did this until I turned sixty in early 2020, when I retired.

Some core principles have stayed with me throughout my journey:

a. Be bold and upfront, regardless of consequences. I have often stood my ground, even with senior leadership.
b. Support your teams relentlessly. I believe in building happy, loyal teams.

c. Stay intellectually curious. Exposure to varied sectors has made me a constant learner—I still read white papers on power, tyres, tea and more, though I have no connection with them anymore.
d. Never offer inducements to journalists. I have always built trust on credibility, not favours.

## 41

# Nitin Thakur

### GLOBAL HEAD - STRATEGIC INITIATIVES & COMMUNICATIONS, OYO

*'I see myself as both a "zero to one" and "minus one to zero" leader.'*

I COME FROM A FAMILY OF MIGRANTS. MY PARENTS LIVED IN undivided Punjab, but both their families were uprooted and forced to migrate during Partition. They were very young when it happened and had to rebuild their lives from scratch. They eventually settled in areas neighbouring Delhi, mainly in Haryana, experiencing the typical struggles of migrant families. My father worked three jobs to provide for the family, while my mother was a teacher. Both were in government service—my father worked across various ministries, from the Planning Commission to the Law Ministry, while my mother taught Hindi and history.

As a child, I witnessed our family's steady progress, mirroring India's own urban growth. I remember the excitement when we got our first scooter, a Lambretta, and the long hours my father worked to ensure we had a comfortable life. I also recall the anticipation of my parents buying their first piece of land where they eventually built our home through loans and sheer determination. Life then was about patience—waiting years for a telephone connection, for example. All this shaped my perspective on career and resilience.

When I completed my schooling at Cambridge School in Delhi, I felt lost. Suddenly, my studies had to align with a career path, but I had no real awareness of my strengths or interests. For a few years, I tried to convince my family to start a business I could eventually manage. I even got involved in a trucking business through family friends, making a small investment. There was a phase where I might have ended up as a transporter. But I was miserable. The culture and way of life in the business world felt completely different from the structured, understated life of a civil service family.

The unrest with the trucking business led me to start a community newspaper where I served as editor, ad sales manager, designer, production lead and distribution manager all at once. While it was profitable due to negligible overhead costs, the growth did not meet the lofty goals I had set. My vision was to launch multiple community newspapers once the model was refined.

Ultimately, I ended up pursuing an MBA—an almost default choice, decided at the last minute. The newspaper idea eventually fell by the wayside when I started B-school. That marked the next chapter of my journey. A new PR consultancy was taking shape—one that would soon become one of India's largest: Vaishnavi. Before Vaishnavi's emergence, no large business group in India had consolidated its PR mandate. It became the PR consultancy for the entire Tata Group, a feat unheard of in those days.

As a result, it quickly became one of India's largest PR consultancies by revenue, within just a few months. I thrived there, spending five years with the firm. Over time, I rose to the position of head of North and East regions, as well as the national practice head for its consumer business. My responsibilities included handling both Tata and non-Tata clients, ranging from Tata Global Beverages (then Tata Tea and Tata Coffee) to Titan. The energy at Vaishnavi was infectious. By the time I exited, the company was also forming Neucom, an independent consultancy that eventually took on the PR mandate for the Reliance Group.

However, I moved on because I got an incredible opportunity at Microsoft. The hiring process took around six to eight months. Interestingly, I was rejected in the final round by the then-country head, Doug Hauger, an American who was exceptionally particular about punctuality. What I presumed to be a polite, courtesy round turned into a rejection, in my reading, primarily because I arrived late for the interview.

I moved on, not thinking much about it, but the team seemed to have liked me. After months of searching for the right candidate, they revisited my application and requested Doug to reconsider. This time, I ensured I arrived at the interview location forty-five minutes early. Before I even joined, I was informed that my hiring manager was leaving. This meant I would be taking on additional responsibilities, reporting directly to Doug. While it was exciting to step into a higher-order role, adjusting to a multinational giant like Microsoft was a challenge. The layers of jargon, complex structures and coordination across product groups, business units, regional and global headquarters—it was an intense learning curve. I worked closely with Meenu Handa, one of the finest communications professionals. After three years at

Microsoft, I started looking for other opportunities. That's when the Max Group came along.

At the time, Max was a leading conglomerate with joint ventures in life insurance, health insurance, hospitals and other industries. Though not the largest in size as far as conglomerates go, it had a strong reputation. I joined at the corporate level, overseeing PR across all subsidiaries. Each business unit had its own PR setup, but my role at the group level positioned me theoretically on the senior side of the communications hierarchy.

But that phase was short-lived. I quickly realised how challenging it is to get things done without a direct reporting structure. Persuasion became my primary tool—I had to influence people to see things from my perspective without any formal authority.

Max turned out to be the longest chapter of my career, spanning over twelve years. I had the opportunity to work closely with the founder, Analjit Singh, and collaborate with multiple CEOs as he transitioned away from daily operations.

But after crossing the ten-year mark, at the age of forty-five, I faced a choice—continue at Max for another fifteen years until retirement or step out of my comfort zone. As much as I loved the company, staying indefinitely felt a bit much. However, making a career move after such a long tenure at a respected conglomerate came with challenges. The market often perceives long-term employees as too embedded in one culture, potentially struggling to adapt to a new environment.

Breaking that perception was not easy, and in situations like these, a personal bridge—a mutual connection—can be crucial. That is where Rohit Kapoor, a former colleague, played a role. Having moved to OYO a year-and-a-half earlier, he reached out about an open head of communications position.

The hiring process at OYO was rigorous: four rounds of interviews, completely independent of Rohit's referral. He simply got me a foot in the door, ensuring I wasn't overlooked due to my unconventional profile. The onus was on me to prove myself.

The first few months were a shock. The pace, the turnaround expectations and the sheer volume of work were unlike anything I had experienced before. The company embraced a culture of rapid execution—launch now, iterate along the way—a stark contrast to Max's meticulous approach, where perfection was the intent from day one.

Crises were common. Just a few months in, I was told we were initiating an IPO process, which multiplied the scrutiny on the company. A year on, after making rapid strides in India, I was given the global mandate. I restructured the team and expanded my scope. Soon, I was pulled into areas beyond PR—what I call the 'backward integration' of PR. What made OYO stand out was its boldness to break barriers.

I see myself as both a 'zero to one' and 'minus one to zero' leader. This means that when there's a fundamental issue affecting OYO's reputation, I take on projects to fix it—regardless of which function it falls under. Conversely, when there is an opportunity to enhance our reputation through strategic pilots in different business areas, I take ownership of those initiatives as well.

At this stage in my career—after thirty years—one might expect to slow down. But the excitement of working for an Indian MNC that is rapidly expanding globally, combined with the freedom to operate without rigid functional boundaries, keeps my energy levels high.

On a personal note, in 2022, my wife wanted our daughter to finish her school and higher education abroad, so they relocated to London. As a result, I now split my time between India and the UK, spending about three to four months working out of London, five to six months in India and the rest travelling internationally for business.

It is quite an unrooted lifestyle for someone who, for the first thirty to thirty-five years of his life, never moved houses and spent nearly thirteen years in a single professional role. For the first time, when asked where I see myself five years from now, I can confidently say, 'I don't know.'

In summary, the past few years have been a whirlwind of growth, learning and transformation. It has been a journey from predictability to unpredictability, and I could not be more excited about what is next.

# 42

# Aparna Thomas

## GLOBAL CORPORATE AFFAIRS LEAD - ESTABLISHED PRODUCTS, SANOFI

*'Public relations is a transformative journey from belief to execution.'*

I WAS BORN AND RAISED IN VADODARA, GUJARAT. I AM A third-generation resident of the city as my paternal grandparents—both in government service—moved there in the 1940s. My grandfather served in the revenue department, while my grandmother was a medical doctor. Because they each had transferable jobs that sometimes took them to different cities and villages, they decided to send both their sons to a boarding school in Mount Abu. My father later did his intermediate studies at St Xavier's College, Mumbai, before returning to Vadodara to pursue his engineering degree.

Meanwhile, my mother who was from Bombay and had done her schooling from Bangalore, aspired to do her master's in clothing and textiles. At that time, MS University was the only institution in India to offer the degree. That's how she came to Vadodara. She later taught at her alma mater, while my father spent the next thirty-five and more years manufacturing and selling batteries for a Japanese firm.

My growing up years were typical of small-town living in a cosmopolitan city. We watched every play hosted by Shakespeare Society and annually took part in the garba festival with equal fervour. We visited art exhibitions at the Fine Arts faculty and watched every Hindi movie before the weekend was up. Everyone knew everyone.

My parents though were and continue to be the strongest influences in my life. Their generation was shaped by the cultural influences of the 1960s, whether it was Elvis Presley, John F. Kennedy or Mehmood. Many of us, raised by parents from that era, were moulded by a mix of these global influences, and while they have never demanded it of me, I strive hard to match their towering influence in my life.

Despite these influences, I followed a simple decision-making process when I joined the Arts faculty at MS University. I loved English literature and reading. I also greatly admired my mother, who as you now know, taught at the university. So, my original career plan was to pursue a PhD and become a professor of English literature.

But that was not meant to be. Though I was a good student, I could not write super-fast and fill supplementary sheets with fluff. So, I did not score enough to get into a PhD programme. The summer I completed my master's was stressful because I really did not know what to do next.

One morning I bumped into a professor from the political science department—someone my parents knew well. He too had a daughter my age, so in passing, asked what my plans were. When I admitted I was unsure, he mentioned a new master's programme in mass communication that was closing applications in a few days. He happened to teach there and encouraged me to apply.

At that time, mass communication was almost synonymous with journalism—I had little idea about the broader scope of the field. As luck would have it, out of thousands of applicants I secured a spot in a batch of just twenty students. During orientation, I remember the professor asking us what we intended to do after we graduated, and nearly everyone said they wanted to be a journalist. But by the end of the degree-course, many—including me—had shifted focus to public relations, radio and other fields.

After my graduation, I knew I had to leave Baroda to truly discover myself. I was twenty-five by then, with two master's degrees, a freelance stint with *The Times of India* group, and little else to show besides it.

After a brief internship at Madison PR in Mumbai, I applied for a job at Corporate Voice (now Weber Shandwick) and got it. The two master's degrees notwithstanding, my starting pay was merely ₹8,000–9,000 per month (in 1999). During the five years with Corporate Voice, I 'graduated' to lead the healthcare and IT verticals for the Mumbai office.

So, what kind of a working professional did I become? One who is authentic, loathes mediocrity and strives for excellence in ideas and execution.

Twenty-five years later, I still want to make my parents proud by creating a body of work that's worth the time, effort and heart I put into it. The only shortcut I take is sometimes calling my father to bounce off words or phrases to deliver impactful messages. It's also a delightful way of staying connected and sharing my work with him.

When it comes to work ethic, the benchmark my parents have set is high. Over time, while building a reputation for products and brands, I have earned a reputation for being authentic and reliable. I cannot emphasise enough the importance of authenticity in the field of PR.

For instance, a long time ago, a whistleblower issue surfaced in one of the organisations I was working for. A reporter had probing questions. I had the facts, but since the company was listed and the matter was under investigation (charges were later dismissed), it was not possible to share details. I navigated through this conversation with a narrative that thankfully aligned with the information the reporter had obtained under the Right to Information Act. As my version corroborated her findings, she knew she could trust my overall narrative. This trust—built on credibility—proved invaluable going forward in my relationship with the journalist fraternity.

That's why I have always been selective about the brands I work for—if I do not believe in them, I cannot represent them with conviction. Authenticity fuels passion, and when combined they create a powerful force capable of making remarkable things happen.

The turning point in my career was in 2003–04, when I worked on the WHO-ORS account and Lifebuoy's Swasthya Chetna campaign and had the opportunity to work on strategic partnerships for impactful outcomes. Before these, I was like any other PR professional with the usual media relations experience. The WHO-ORS campaign was aimed at central Indian states—Bihar, Madhya Pradesh, Uttar Pradesh, Rajasthan and Delhi—where diarrhoea-related dehydration amongst children under five years was a significant public health issue. Awareness alone was not enough; healthcare communications had to drive behaviour change. It was not just about publishing informational articles in newspapers; we needed to ensure people acted.

This was also the time when the concept of incentive-based PR retainers was emerging. Instead of a fixed monthly fee, consultancies were given a base retainer (say, ₹1.5–2 lakh per month instead of ₹3 lakh maybe) and an incentive-based fee to meet specific campaign goals. Typically, PR outcomes are perceived as nebulous because the outcome can be seen only over time. However, brand managers work to deliver sales targets for the quarter and the year. They need to see value for their investment in PR *now*.

So, the incentive fee model pushed us to deliver measurable impact, proving to be a significant step in bringing more revenue into the consultancy firm.

In the spirit of authenticity, let me share an anecdote demonstrating something that did not work as planned. I was attempting to forge a partnership between Lifebuoy and Brihanmumbai Municipal Corporation (BMC) to place handwash-related messages in public toilets. BMC assumed that Lifebuoy had a transactional and commercial agenda. Over several meetings, we reiterated that the initiative was purely educational. Eventually, we backed off.

However, a couple of months later, the BMC put several large hoardings on Marine Drive, Mumbai, about waste segregation and unexpectedly included Lifebuoy's branding to indicate that it was a joint message. I'm not sure why they decided to do the 'joint-branding', but since the campaign execution was conducted without consent or discussion, we requested them to remove the hoardings. Ironically, this incident finally helped the BMC realise that the brand was genuinely promoting public health.

My tool for success is that I must genuinely believe in the campaign, the purpose and the message. Accordingly, I have handpicked my team and consultancy and event partners.

Excellence is a natural outcome only when we challenge each other, push each other and partner with each other with shared values and purpose. This way, we earn each other's respect and thrive on the success we deliver together.

Ultimately, PR is a transformative journey from belief to execution, from collaboration to partnerships and from transcending briefs to transforming people's lives.

# 43

# Varghese Thomas

### GLOBAL HEAD - COMMUNICATIONS, MARKETING & SOCIAL MEDIA, TATA ELECTRONICS

---

*'Whether you're choosing to pitch a bold idea or facing a crisis that could go viral for all the wrong reasons, it is key to stay calm and make tough calls.'*

I WAS BORN AND RAISED IN NEW DELHI IN A MIDDLE-INCOME family. Academically, I was an average student. My true passion lay in sports. From an early age, I was an enthusiastic sportsperson, participating in athletics, soccer and badminton. I had the privilege of representing my school, college and university in various sports and even competed in the Delhi State Athletics Championship. Sports taught me invaluable lessons about teamwork, resilience and the importance of connection—skills that would later become pivotal in my career.

I completed my bachelor's degree from Delhi University, followed by a master's in business administration. My professional journey began in an American project financing firm, where I worked on feasibility studies. But it was by accident that I transitioned into PR. I started in business development at a leading PR consultancy, and the journey into PR turned out to be both challenging and thrilling.

Over time, I came to understand the power of strategic messaging and the importance of building lasting relationships with clients, media and audiences. I was fortunate to work with some exceptional consultancies before transitioning to the corporate world, where I spent twenty-five years working with global brands like Intel, Cisco, BlackBerry and TVS Motor.

As a communications leader, I have come to realise that success is about much more than just delivering messages. It's about having a strategic vision—aligning messaging with organisational goals and anticipating challenges like a chess master plotting five moves ahead. It's also about being a collaborator, creating a space where diverse ideas can thrive and where the team's collective creativity can work magic. After all, great ideas often come from the most unexpected places, like that one person in the meeting who's convinced that 'hashtag' is a form of punctuation.

The ability to take decisions under pressure and take risks is crucial. There is no 'safe bet' in PR. Whether you're choosing to pitch a bold idea or facing a crisis that could go viral for all the wrong reasons, it is key to stay calm and make tough calls. And yes, it helps if you're not afraid to embrace a little chaos.

And beyond these professional qualities, a successful communications leader treats everyone with kindness and respect. They understand the power of human connection and aim to be a leader who leaves a lasting, positive impact—not scars—by inspiring others and guiding the organisation's narrative with clarity, confidence and compassion.

This is the essence of leadership in communications: a combination of vision, empathy and courage, all directed towards building a positive, lasting legacy for the organisation and its people.

I have been fortunate to be associated with some outstanding campaigns. I would like to recount a few of them here.

First, when I was a new business development person at the consultancy, we were pitching for the Eurocopter account, a leading helicopter manufacturing company. I was tasked with creating a SWOT analysis and a competition report as part of our strategy for the pitch. The challenge, however, was that the helicopter manufacturing industry was incredibly niche, and reliable information was hard to come by.

Undeterred, I threw myself into the task, diving deep into research from all available sources—some more unconventional than others. The process was not without its risks and looking back, it was probably a little dangerous. However, I managed to gather not just a competitive analysis but a comprehensive understanding of the challenges and the unique opportunities it presented for the client.

I will not go into the details of how I gathered some of that information, but let us just say it required a fair amount of creativity, risk-taking and persistence. In the end, it paid off—our proposal was thorough, well-researched and gave the client actionable insights. And yes, we did win the account. That experience taught me a lot about the importance of resourcefulness, perseverance and thinking out of the box when it comes to winning big pitches.

Second, the BlackBerry crisis in India in 2010 was a defining moment for our PR team as we navigated significant challenges on multiple fronts. The Indian government raised national security concerns, demanding access to encrypted messages sent via BlackBerry devices. The pressure was immense, with the threat of a complete shutdown of services in India—one of our key markets—looming large. On top of this, a global server outage lasting three days exacerbated the situation, causing widespread concern among users and media alike.

We had to manage both crises simultaneously, with media scrutiny at an all-time high. Our primary objective was to maintain transparency and reassure both the government and the public. We worked closely with the Indian authorities, negotiating a resolution that balanced security concerns with privacy protection while also keeping the media informed of the progress. At the same time, we focused on downplaying the server outage incident, assuring customers that we were actively resolving the issue and that it would not affect their experience going forward.

By maintaining open communication, providing clear messaging and addressing concerns head-on, we were able to defuse the crisis. Despite the challenges, our strategic approach helped us avoid a total shutdown, safeguard BlackBerry's reputation and ultimately restore customer trust in India and globally.

Lastly, one of the most challenging moments I faced at Cisco occurred when a major corporate announcement—a strategic investment partnership—was leaked to the media on the morning of our planned announcement. The news-break threw the PR team into turmoil, threatening to derail the carefully crafted narrative we had spent weeks preparing.

Our immediate focus was on managing the narrative and ensuring maximum media coverage. We quickly pivoted, reaching out to critical journalists and influencers with exclusive insights while using every available platform—press releases, social media, internal communications and one-on-one briefings—to control the story.

What initially seemed like a crisis turned into an opportunity. By acting swiftly and strategically, we generated some of the most extensive and positive media coverage Cisco had ever seen. The experience underscored the importance of agility in PR and reinforced the value of strong media relationships. In the end, the leaked news became one of the most talked-about stories in the business, transforming a potential setback into a major win.

## 44

# Aman Ullah

### Head - Corporate Media, Asia & Middle East, HSBC

*'A quiet certainty fills me on how ready I am to take on whatever comes next.'*

I WAS BORN AND RAISED IN COLABA, MUMBAI, BY A SINGLE mother, who worked hard to ensure a decent life for us. Growing up, my siblings and I did not have much, but we always had books. My mother believed a solid education ensured a good life. Reading was non-negotiable. We read the daily newspaper and deliberated on the day's events—a tradition I still uphold. Little did I know then that I was creating the groundwork for the future.

While I was preparing to be a banker, life threw a curveball. My mother received a terminal diagnosis. Overnight, I became one of the caregivers, while managing responsibilities, including taking up casual jobs for extra income. She passed away the year I graduated from university.

That period was beyond tough. What kept us moving forward were her teachings, especially hard work, commitment, adaptability and resilience. Those lessons are still my guiding force in life, woven into every choice.

It was around this time that law captivated me. Also, the college offered morning classes, allowing me to work in the day. This seemed ideal. In the first week of my life at Elphinstone College, I walked into HDFC Ltd, which was located right behind college, to inquire about opportunities. They had an opening in the communications department. For the next couple of years, I worked on the launch of multiple joint ventures, financial results, AGMs, ADR listing, community initiatives (CSR) and annual reports, calendars, newsletters, visiting cards and signages, among others. You name it, I did it. This experience led me to my life's true calling—communications.

Although I had direct exposure and experience in communications, I wanted to explore it in a structured manner. Guess it traces back to my mother's doctrine of requiring a solid education. The shift from law to communications was a transformative decision that set me firmly on the path to a career I will always be passionate about.

I enrolled for an evening programme in communications at XIC, Mumbai, while continuing to work for HDFC. Life was chaotic but rewarding. One day, the course director spoke about working outside our comfort zone. It got me thinking. My job was comfortable and secure with a flattened learning curve. I realised that a consultancy experience was essential to become a versatile PR professional.

Walking away from HDFC was one of the hardest decisions I made but was the right one. My next two stints—Coffee Communications and LinOpinion—offered a steep and stimulating learning curve. My experiences with different domains steered me to my interest—the financial sector. The banker within me was not gone after all!

I joined Perfect Relations to expand their corporate and financial services practice. My responsibilities included managing client relationships, media relations and leading business growth. During this time, I also began a new personal chapter by marrying the love of my life, my long-time girlfriend.

The next decade was a fast-paced whirl. The firm had a remarkably open culture. They encouraged growth, experimentation and the free exchange of ideas, thanks to then CEO Valerie Pinto and my manager, Rohan Kanchan. We grew from a five-member team handling five accounts to over twenty professionals servicing over thirty accounts. We were engaged in every pitch in the marketplace. It was a period of immense personal growth and learning, working alongside a highly energetic and passionate team. Today many of them are at senior positions across Asia Pacific and Europe, demonstrating the same energy and passion.

I have countless examples of client interactions and lessons learnt over my decade with Perfect Relations. Every day, I learnt something new to gain a fresh perspective and challenge myself. The 2008 financial crisis prompted me to manage accounts outside the finance industry, like international luxury automotive brands, port operators, logistics companies, law firms and even a professional diving company. I strived to become their on-ground specialist, guiding them through their decision making. I have managed logistics and media drives and dealt with last-minute mix-ups, such as missed flights and misplaced bags. It's led to strong operational skills and lasting relationships with the media.

Another memory is managing a crisis for a foreign bank facing a case of major fraud. It was a high-pressure environment, working with stakeholders from across the world. The experience expanded my understanding of crisis management, risk assessment and governance. My background in law helped me navigate the complexities of the situation.

Amid this, the education bug bit me. I went back to college to gain a master's degree in financial management without quitting my job. My managers were most supportive. Between work, college and home, it was a roller-coaster ride. I credit my wife for keeping me sane and moving forward through this period.

Of course, no reflection on Perfect Relations would be complete without the mention of the indomitable Dilip Cherian. I must share an instance that left a lasting impact on me. This was almost two decades ago. Dilip was conducting a workshop with fifteen young FMCG brand managers. He opened with an unexpected question, 'How many of you know Mandarin?' Not a single hand went up. Nobody seemed perturbed. He explained, 'Your biggest competitor is going to be China. Ten years from now, you'll either be selling to or buying from them.'

His foresight still resonates with me. Working alongside people with such forward-thinking perspectives fundamentally shaped my outlook to consider the bigger picture. Always.

I still remember how Perfect Relations was amongst the first consultancy to form a dedicated online PR and crisis team. This was in 2009. While the profession was waking up to the speed of digital backlash, we were proactively managing reputational risks and setting new standards. Also, another example—all account managers had to work closely with the public affairs and policy teams. This alignment ensured we showed up coordinated and credible in front of lawmakers, regulators and advocacy groups.

Learning to predict the future, rather than simply reacting to the present has been a valuable lesson in my career. This thought process is crucial when you work with the C-suite.

One day, over an interaction, the client's business card caught my eye. His office was on the fifty-first floor in a building in Hong Kong. For days, I mused about the view from his office. For me, until this point, I functioned within the five kilometres from home radius—be it school, colleges or my workplaces. Not by design, just a stroke of luck! Now, I was aspiring to step away outside this radius.

Then, HSBC happened. Although it was within the same radius, the profile (head of communications, India) was exciting. One of the most significant lessons of this transition was adapting from a consultancy mindset—where the focus was on providing multiple options and ideas—to an in-house role, which called for a more concentrated effort, prioritising the top initiatives that would yield the most value to the organisation. Most importantly, I made the decisions. It was my responsibility.

This required a comprehensive understanding of complex banking terminology, evolving market dynamics, competitive factors, intricate processes and the compliance and regulatory framework, among other aspects. I had to pivot quickly with no time to linger. Thus, you come to trust the expertise of those around you—whether they're part of your team, external specialists or even junior colleagues—to get things done. It's all about learning to collaborate and embracing true teamwork. Another bonus, I could spend more time with my toddler, as home was a short walk away. Proximity ensured some balance in my work life.

In late 2022, I finally moved to Hong Kong, bag and baggage with wife and daughter for my current role with the bank's regional headquarters. I'm involved in driving the bank's global reputation and positioning across Asia and now the Middle East. Finally, the business card ambition has become a reality!

Right now, the C-suite must navigate unpredictable global economy and geopolitical situations, technological disruptions and innovations, the changing media landscape with new platforms and channels and build a strong and inclusive team while managing stakeholders and driving business growth. This list is not exhaustive. Communications is at the heart of making this happen. We are a core function, with an equal seat at the table alongside business. More than ever before, the C-suite expect it!

Times are changing. And times are certainly exciting. A quiet certainty fills me on how ready I am to take on whatever comes next.

# 45

# Shaily Vaswani

## SVP - Group Communications & Brand, Aditya Birla Group

*'From law to fashion, from journalism to corporate communications—my journey has been a story of reinvention, resilience and the power of embracing change.'*

I GREW UP IN MUMBAI, IN A HOME FILLED WITH WARMTH, discipline and aspirations. My father, a principled estate agent, and my mother, the heart of our home, instilled in me the values of hard work and perseverance. Academically inclined, I was expected to pursue medicine, but my heart was set on law. However, life had other plans. Limited opportunities in Mumbai and my father's reluctance to let me study elsewhere led me to explore alternatives.

I enrolled at Jai Hind College, still nurturing my legal aspirations. But at twenty, marriage altered my trajectory. Instead of letting my ambitions fade, I adapted. I pivoted towards fashion journalism, graduating as a topper from

India International Trade Center (IITC) Bombay. This led to freelance work with publications like the Clothing Manufacturers Association of India (CMAI) magazine, where I had the privilege of interviewing industry stalwarts. Under the mentorship of the legendary late Shabari Dhol, I honed my storytelling skills and discovered my love for communication.

Teaching soon became another unexpected avenue. I was invited to IITC as a faculty member, designing advanced courses in fashion journalism, merchandising and window dressing. A move to Pune post-marriage exposed me to advertising, media and corporate communications. One thing led to another, and soon, I found myself deeply immersed in the world of branding and storytelling.

A pivotal moment came when I joined TASMAC, a behavioural training organisation. Initially sceptical, I embraced the challenge and developed training programmes on presentation skills, emotional intelligence and internal communication. This experience set the stage for my entry into corporate communications. In 2000, I joined the Mahindra Group during a critical period of organisational transformation. My role in internal communications quickly expanded to acquisitions, employee engagement and marketing communications, solidifying my expertise in the field.

Relocating to Mumbai while my family remained in Pune was not easy. Juggling a high-intensity career while being a 'weekend mom' required immense support from my family. My mother-in-law and husband ensured stability at home, allowing me to chase my professional aspirations.

My next chapter brought me to Tata Communications during its transformation from VSNL. Being part of such a massive rebranding effort was exhilarating. It meant long hours, extended stays away from home and a crash course in managing large-scale corporate transitions. It was also the phase where I had the privilege of working with Samira Kohli, the APAC head of marketing communication, who had a reputation for being a tough taskmaster and a perfectionist. Our relationship evolved into a silent mentorship that continues to this day.

From Tata Communications, I then moved to Aegis (an ESSAR Group company), where I got the opportunity to manage a global profile. I was responsible for branding, rebranding, internal and external communications, PR and Media across sixteen acquisitions in just three years — an experience that tested and refined my skills in global communications. The experience of managing acquisitions, leading communications for one of Saudi Arabia's largest joint venture deals of 2011 and leading a diverse team across four continents further enhanced my capabilities as a communications expert.

Following Aegis, I led internal communications at JP Morgan's India Global Contact Centre. While the stint at JP Morgan was a short one, I got the opportunity to work on high-impact employee engagement initiatives like the Lace Up marathon and drafting the mission statement for the Global Contact Centre (GCC). This was followed by my stint at VFS Global, where I managed PR, crisis communication and internal engagement across the US, Europe, the Middle East, Southeast Asia and Russia. The role required close collaboration with governments, embassies and consulates, adding a whole new dimension to my communication experience.

Then came the Aditya Birla Group, where I have now been for seven enriching years. When I joined, Dr Pragnya Ram entrusted me with branding responsibilities for Aditya Birla Group (ABG). One of my earliest projects — the 'Big in Your

Life' campaign—launched within four months and set the tone for the work to come. Needless to say, working under Dr Ram has been one of the most defining experiences of my career.

As the baton passed to Sandeep Gurumurthi, my role evolved further. Over the last six years, his empowering leadership and trust in the team have allowed me to take on broader mandates—strengthening internal communications, leading digital narratives and building communication assets. It's the kind of environment every professional hopes for: one that encourages initiative, rewards clarity of thought and gives you the room to grow.

As I reflect on this journey—spanning three decades, five industries and countless lessons—I'm reminded that the most enduring wisdom often comes not from milestones, but from the moments in between. Here are a few truths that have stayed with me and might resonate with others walking their own winding paths.

1. *Embrace reinvention*: Career paths are rarely linear. Every detour can be a doorway to discovering a new strength or passion.
2. *Stay curious, always*: Whether it's fashion journalism or global branding, curiosity fuels growth. Never stop learning.
3. *Find power in storytelling*: Beyond strategy and structure, communication is ultimately about connection and meaning.
4. *Do not fear change—lead it*: From corporate transformations to personal pivots, be the steady voice in the storm.
5. *Seek mentors—and listen*: Leaders do not just shape careers—they shape character.

6. *Balance ambition with empathy*: Leadership is not just about results, but about people, purpose and presence.
7. *Make resilience your superpower*: Long commutes, high-pressure roles and personal sacrifices—persistence matters.
8. *Know your worth—then own your voice*: Especially as a woman in leadership, confidence and clarity go hand in hand.
9. *Lead with quiet conviction*: You do not have to be the loudest in the room. Steady, thoughtful leadership leaves a deeper mark.
10. *Give back by lifting others*: Mentor, support and celebrate the next generation. Legacy is not just what you do but what you enable.

# 46

# Pradeep Wadhwa

FORMER DIRECTOR - CORPORATE COMMUNICATIONS, PEPSICO INDIA

---

*'Lifelong learning has always been a personal priority. I make it a point to stay hands-on with emerging technologies.'*

I HAVE ALWAYS BEEN ROOTED IN DELHI. UNLIKE MANY PEERS who studied or worked abroad, my entire education was in the national capital. I grew up in a well-educated household—my father was an engineer, my mother a teacher. I was an above-average student: never a topper, but never in trouble either. A steady, uneventful academic path.

In the 1980s and 1990s, scoring in the 80–90 per cent range was considered exceptional. I completed my BSc and MSc in Physics from Hansraj College, Delhi University. But by the end of my master's, I realised I did not want to teach or become a scientist. Civil services did not appeal to me either. The pre-Y2K era saw many opting for a master's in computer application (MCA). I had the maths skills for it, but I preferred working with people over machines. That realisation led me to pursue an MBA from BIMTECH.

After completing my MBA, I began my career in marketing at Berger Paints but quickly realised the work there did not excite me. My earlier internship at HTA (now JWT) had already shown me that advertising was not my calling either. Coming from a non-IIM background, breaking into top-tier marketing roles at big companies was also a challenge.

Around that time, a senior introduced me to someone from a PR firm. The way they described the role made it sound meaningful—though, in hindsight, a bit overhyped. Still, it piqued my interest enough to make the switch. In 1999, I joined Perfect Relations—then a leading PR firm—as an assistant manager, leveraging my MBA and prior experience to bypass the entry level.

At the time, Perfect Relations was expanding into specialised verticals. I joined the Image Inc division, where I handled infrastructure clients. It was a period of high-stakes, high-impact work—campaigns like the Dabhol Power Project, India's first privatisation with BALCO and the COAI vs. Reliance case during their controversial telecom entry. The learning curve was steep and the exposure invaluable.

After three years, however, I found myself increasingly typecast as the 'crisis guy', with most assignments rooted in crisis or infrastructure. Not wanting to be boxed into that niche, I moved to Weber Shandwick (then Corporate Voice | Weber Shandwick) to focus on brand communications. But thanks to my physics background, I soon gravitated toward tech clients, leading mandates for Oracle, Hitachi, Agilent Technologies and others.

I later spent about a year and a half at Genesis BCW (now Burson India), managing marquee accounts like PepsiCo, HP, HCL Tech and Vodafone.

In 2009, I returned to Weber Shandwick as the general manager for the Delhi office, a role I held for about a year. Around the same time, PepsiCo was searching for a new head of PR. Given that Genesis BCW was already servicing the account, a direct approach was not appropriate. However, through mutual connections, I was introduced to the team and eventually joined PepsiCo as the head of communications for India. After seven years in this role, I went on to lead Brand PR and Partner Communications across Asia, the Middle East and North Africa. It was a transformative period, both professionally and personally.

In 2017, I moved to ReNew Power, India's leading renewable energy company founded by Sumant Sinha. I spent two years there, building the brand from the ground up and positioning Sumant as a key voice in the sector. I had joined with a clear plan to eventually branch out on my own—and after two fulfilling years, that's exactly what I did.

In late 2019, after a brief break, I launched Kritical Edge—a communications consultancy with a clear focus on internal communications, leadership messaging and digital engagement. The intent was to break away from the conventional media relations-heavy PR model and explore more strategic, future-facing avenues.

In the aftermath of COVID-19, I experimented with alternative business models, including taking equity stakes in start-ups in exchange for marketing and communication services. While some ventures showed promise, others folded or failed to honour agreements. It was a tough but valuable lesson in navigating trust and accountability outside the structured environment of large organisations.

Lifelong learning has always been a personal priority. I make it a point to stay hands on with emerging technologies, especially AI and digital tools, often diving in myself first so I can effectively upskill my team.

# Afterword

A S IN THE PREVIOUS TWO BOOKS, WE WOULD LIKE TO THANK our parents, our spouses and our daughters (Sia, Saisha and Swara) besides our colleagues (Roshan, Anubhuti, Ameeta and Joulyn) and the team at Westland (Karthika, Aurodeep, Amrita and Saurabh) for always being there.

We would also like to thank some professionals who played a role in our careers by way of our own story that brings their name to the fore.

*Sarika Chavan:*

I was born and raised in Mumbai. Both my parents hail from Mangalore.

My father worked at Tata Steel, and my mother was a homemaker. I am the youngest of three children. I studied at Nazareth School in Bhayander and and graduated in botany from Jai Hind College at Churchgate. I have a diploma in public relations from the Xavier Institute of Communications and a two-year postgraduate diploma in marketing from the Welingkar Institute of Management.

## Afterword

I worked at Efunds, one of the leading BPOs then, after my graduation. My first stint in PR began when I interned with Farid Currim at Red Pepper Communications while pursuing my post-graduation course at XIC in 2003. I owe my initial learnings to Farid, as he would insist that I go for media rounds every single day. Post that, I began working at Perfect Relations, which was led by Dilip Cherian and Bobby Kewalramani and helmed by Valerie Pinto along with Rohan Kanchan and Shashikant Someshwar. My life here was much easier thanks to Farid's persistent support and guidance.

After a six-year stint at Perfect Relations, I decided to pause my corporate career to focus on my two daughters, which was a very rewarding two years. I then decided to get back to the office life and worked for the next two years at Text100 (now Archetype) under the watch of Ketan Jain, Sonia Mansata and Sunayna Malik. This then led me to Adfactors PR where, thanks to the vision of Rajesh Chaturvedi and Madan Bahal, I got the opportunity to work on some of India's finest brands guided by Percy Dubash.

After seven years at Adfactors PR, my final corporate job before I chose to branch out on my own was as a vice president at Weber Shandwick. My gratitude goes out to my professors at XIC, Vinod Srivastava, Rajeev Chawla and S. Sudarshan for instilling in me the love for the profession.

Another significant avenue I traversed was writing a monthly book review since 2021. As of 2025, I have written over fifty reviews and counting. I also am co-creating a network of corporate communications and public relations professionals focused on learning under the aegis of the South Asian Public Relations Alliance (SAPRA). One of the things that gives me immense joy is working on retreats for CCOs. These include Assembly and Manifest, with more to come.

I currently run a social impact venture, Sparkle Gift Cards, which is making a difference in the lives of thousands of beneficiaries through our NGO partners.

I would also like to express my heartfelt gratitude to my partner and mentor, Amith Prabhu, for inspiring me both personally and professionally. His unwavering belief in getting things done and his ability to instil in me a go-getter attitude have shaped the person I am today. I owe much of my journey to his constant support and guidance.

My philosophy is to live and let live. With this formula I have managed to be a happy person both personally and professionally.

*Amith Prabhu:*

I was born and raised in Mangalore, a coastal town in South Karnataka. My father was a college professor, and my mother was a high school teacher. I was the older of two boys. I studied at St Aloysius School and Pre-University College in Mangalore. I enrolled in the SDM Law College of the Mangalore University for my graduation and completed my master's in public relations at the Symbiosis Institute of Media and Communication, Pune.

After completing my undergraduate studies, I took up a one-year assignment to travel across the country on a voluntary project to promote the UN's International Year of the Volunteers in 2001. After my postgraduate studies, I wanted to be based in the national capital region and chose to work at Genesis Public Relations (now Burson India) in Gurgaon as part of an interesting initiative called the Associate

Learning Programme (ALP), which was a unique management training initiative led by Prema Sagar and Ashwani Singla.

After three eventful years across three locations, I moved to APCO Worldwide as the first employee of the Mumbai office under the guidance of Amit Misra. Thereafter, at age twenty-nine, I got hired as the head of corporate communications of VivaKi (now Publicis Media), where I spent two years under the supervision of Ravi Kiran and later Srikant Shastri and CVL Srinivas. In 2011, I got very lucky to secure a job in Edelman Chicago thanks to Rick Murray, who responded to a tweet and a LinkedIn message.

While I was in the United States, I had the opportunity to attend several high-quality public relations conferences. They left a lasting impression on me, and I thought, 'Why don't we have something like this in India for the PR fraternity?' Inspired, I turned to social media and casually asked if we should create an event for Indian PR professionals. A handful of responses came in with an enthusiastic yes. That's how PRAXIS was born, with the first edition in November 2012. And the rest is history. It is now one of the largest gatherings of its kind without ever having repeated a keynote speaker or a host city over twelve editions.

I returned to India in January 2014. Under the aegis of the Promise Foundation, I continued to build more platforms including Reputation Today and Fulcrum Awards; retreats such as Assembly and Manifest; conferences such as Quorum, Reprise and Spectra; conclaves such as Fiesta, Gravity, Huddle and IndeComms. I co-authored a book during the lockdown, *The Pursuit of Reputation*, with Sujit Patil, and this series with Sarika Chavan followed soon after.

The two highlights of the last decade are co-creating the School of Communications and Reputation under the mentorship of N.S. Rajan, Nitin Mantri and Sonya Madeira.

# Afterword

During the pandemic, like many others, I found myself reflecting on how we could do things differently—how we might give back to society in a new, impactful way. One idea that kept playing in my mind was about creating a charity gift card. The concept was simple: instead of gifting material items to people who already had enough, what if we could channel that generosity towards meaningful causes? The idea of giving back came to me very early in life. Whether it was offering my time, sharing ideas pro bono, or contributing from my own savings, I was always driven by a desire to give back in some way. That spirit naturally extended into my professional journey as well. The result was Sparkle Gift Cards (sparklegiftcards.com), for which I have partnered with Roshan and Sarika.

I often say this—I consider myself incredibly lucky. Yes, I have faced setbacks, but in hindsight, they have been relatively minor compared to those of many others I know. And more importantly, each of those setbacks came with a lesson. Each one opened a new door, offered a new perspective or nudged me in the direction I was meant to go. So, when I say I'm lucky, I do not mean it in a superficial way. To me, luck is the outcome of four key traits: passion, focus, consistency and discipline. If you have these four qualities at the core, luck finds you. And when it does, it brings with it opportunities, resources and people who can shape your journey in extraordinary ways. And to every young person I say this: be safe, be nice, be good and be kind. Safety in every possible way by being mindful, nice to make the world a better place, good to yourself, mentally and physically and kindness to those who can do nothing in return. This belief system drives me.

# The Communication Catalysts
(arranged in alphabetical order by second name)

Amrit Ahuja

Arpana Ahuja

Seema Ahuja

Nazeeb Arif

Sanjay Arora

Melissa Arulappan

Roma Balwani

Rohit Bansal

Sudeep Bhalla

Ophira Bhatia

Nandini Chatterjee

Paresh Chaudhry

Paroma Roy Chowdhury

Madhu Chhibber

Shravani Dang

Anuj Dayal

Deepa Dey

Meenu Handa

Mahesh Jayaram

Ritu Jhingon

Narahari K.S.

Bharatendu Kabi

Manish Kalghatgi

Himanshu Kapadia

Sanjiv Kataria

Raza Khan

Alpana Killawala

Rakhee Lalvani

Nivedeeta Moirangthem

Subhayu Mishra

Rachana Panda

Sujit Patil

Ramya Rajagopalan

Mukund Rajan

Pragnya Ram

Senjam Raj Sekhar

Debasis Ray

Minari Shah

Amandeep Singh

Atul Takle

Nitin Thakur

Aparna Thomas

Varghese Thomas

Aman Ullah

Shaily Vaswani

Pradeep Wadhwa

Sarika Chavan

Amith Prabhu